THE POWER OF SELF-LOVE FOR WOMEN

Practical Steps to Silence Your Inner Critic, Boost Self-Esteem, and Heal from Past Traumas to Achieve Inner Peace & Lasting Happiness

MIYUKI SUGIURA

CONTENTS

INTRODUCTION

Looking in the mirror at a time in my life felt like facing an enemy. Each glance reminded me of how I believed I didn't measure up. The harsh words of my inner critic echoed louder than any praise. It was a struggle to find even a sliver of self-worth. I know that many of you reading this have felt the same way. It's a universal experience yet profoundly personal and isolating.

This book exists to change that narrative. "The Power of Self-Love for Women" is a compassionate guide designed to help you silence that inner critic. It aims to boost your self-esteem and heal those wounds from past traumas. It's about finding inner peace and lasting happiness.

My vision for this book is simple yet profound. I want to equip you with practical tools and strategies to foster self-love and resilience. These are lofty ideals and actionable steps you can start implementing today. This journey is about strengthening your relationship with yourself and overcoming the obstacles that impede your personal growth and well-being.

The structure of this book is designed to guide you through these steps thoughtfully and engagingly. Each chapter focuses on a key theme related to self-love and self-esteem. From understanding the roots of your inner critic to building a daily practice of self-compassion, each section offers insights and strategies you can apply in your life.

Throughout its pages, several vital practices are repeatedly mentioned. These include mindfulness exercises that involve taking deep breaths and focusing on the present moment, daily gratitude affirmations, and embracing the belief that infinite love resides within you, empowering you as you engage with it. These concepts are not randomly placed but are strategically dispersed throughout to deeply embed them in your consciousness by the time you finish reading.

The book includes actionable steps and real-life stories to make the content relatable and impactful. These stories are from women who have walked this path before you. They demonstrate that transformation is possible and that you are not alone in your journey.

At the end of each subchapter, you'll find a section called "Mini Actions You Can Take". These are practical steps you can start practicing today. There's no need to try them all—choose the ones that interest you and give them a try.

Your heart may feel dried and cracked from past hurts, traumas, harsh words from others, guilt from past mistakes, or a lack of confidence in your appearance or personality. However, when you learn to love yourself fully, your confidence will grow, you'll smile more often, and your mood will lighten. Once fully nourished, your heart will overflow with love like a spring, and you'll find yourself sharing that love with those around you.

Remember, you are not alone on this journey. You walk with a Higher Power that resides within you, endowed with infinite love and strength. This Higher Power will protect, encourage, teach, guide, and wrap you in love. It is aware of all your thoughts and emotions. Therefore, practice speaking to this great power daily and seek its help on your journey. Rest assured, the Higher Power will surely assist you.

So, dear reader, I invite you to embark on this journey with me. Let's delve into the steps to quiet your inner critic, elevate your self-esteem, and recover from past traumas.

This is your journey of self-love and transformation, and it begins now. The road ahead may be challenging, but it also promises incredible rewards. You deserve love, particularly from yourself. You are worthy of a life filled with inner peace and enduring happiness. Let's take this journey together, one step at a time.

CHAPTER 1

UNDERSTANDING SELF-LOVE AND ITS IMPORTANCE

One evening, after a long day, I sat alone, overwhelmed by a flood of negative thoughts. I had a loving family and friends who cared for me. Yet, I felt an emptiness that gnawed at my self-worth. It's a paradox many women face: even if you have all the external markers of success, you still feel unworthy.

This moment of vulnerability led me to realize the profound lack of self-love in my life. It wasn't about what I had achieved but how I saw myself. If you've ever felt this way, know you're not alone. This chapter is here to help you understand what self-love truly means and why it matters so much.

1.1 DEFINING SELF-LOVE: WHAT IT IS AND WHY IT MATTERS

Self-love is often misunderstood or needs clarification with other concepts like self-care or self-esteem. At its core, self-love is the unconditional acceptance of oneself. It means embracing who you are, with all your strengths and imperfections. Unlike self-esteem, which can fluctuate based on achievements and external validation, self-love remains constant. It's about appreciating yourself regardless of circumstances. Self-love isn't just about treating yourself to a spa day or buying something nice. Those are acts of self-care, which are important but different. Self-love goes more profound; it's about holistically nurturing your emotional, mental, and physical well-being.

The importance of self-love cannot be overstated. It forms the foundation for healthy relationships. When you love yourself, you set the standard for how others should treat you.

Self-love also plays a crucial role in personal growth and resilience. It gives you the strength to face challenges and bounce back from setbacks. Self-love significantly benefits your mental health. It reduces anxiety and depression, fostering a sense of inner peace and overall happiness. Think of self-love as the root system of a tree. The tree cannot stand tall without solid roots, no matter how many branches it has.

Consider the story of a woman who just had a baby. Her body has changed, and she struggles with accepting her new self. By practicing self-love, she learns to appreciate her body for what it has accomplished rather than how it looks. She starts to focus on her health and well-being rather than societal standards. This perspective shift helps her silence her inner critic and embrace her new identity as a mother.

Another example is a woman who habitually engages in negative self-talk. She constantly berates herself for not being good enough. Through self-love, she begins recognizing these patterns and actively replaces negative thoughts with positive affirmations. This transformation doesn't happen overnight, but with consistent effort, she starts to see herself in a new light.

Mini Actions You Can Take: 1.1

What are you dissatisfied with right now? Are there any aspects of your personality or thinking that you don't like? You might need more time for hobbies, rest, or exercise. You might also not be eating a well-balanced diet. Your decisiveness and ability to take action are lacking. Please write this down on the first page of your journal as the starting line for a journey filled with self-love. Let's improve this situation together, step by step.

1.2 FOUNDATION OF SELF-LOVE: YOU ARE A ONE-OF-A-KIND MASTERPIECE

You are a unique masterpiece, the only one of its kind, created by a great power as its finest work. If you belittle yourself, you are disparaging the 'masterpiece' that your creator made.

A baby cannot do anything by itself. Does that mean a baby is worthless? Of course not. Even if it can't do anything, its mere existence has value.

A human's worth is not determined by their ability to do things.

You are an irreplaceable masterpiece, the finest work of art, simply by being alive.

Therefore, love yourself wholeheartedly. There is no one else like you anywhere in the world. Fully enjoy being such a precious masterpiece created by a great power!

Loving yourself impacts mental health outcomes.

Studies have found that individuals who practice self-love experience fewer symptoms of anxiety and depression. This is because self-love encourages a positive self-image and reduces the need for external validation. When you love yourself, you are less likely to compare yourself unfavorably to others, which can lead to feelings of inadequacy and despair. This aligns with findings from the National Institutes of Health, which indicate that higher levels of self-compassion are linked to increased happiness, optimism, and emotional resilience.

The psychological benefits of self-love are extensive. For starters, it boosts self-esteem and confidence. When you practice self-love, you recognize your worth independent of achievements or others' opinions. This internal validation strengthens your self-esteem, making it more stable and less susceptible to fluctuations. Additionally, self-love reduces anxiety and depression symptoms.

By fostering a positive relationship with yourself, you create a mental environment that is less conducive to negative thinking. This shift can improve emotional regulation, allowing you to manage emotions more effectively.

Emotionally, self-love offers a wealth of benefits. One of the most significant is greater inner peace and contentment. When you accept and love yourself unconditionally, you experience fewer inner conflicts and more harmony. This state of peace makes it easier to cope with setbacks and failures. Instead of berating yourself for mistakes, you can view them as opportunities for growth.

Self-love also strengthens your emotional bonds with others. By setting a standard for treating yourself, you teach others to respect and love you similarly. This mutual respect forms the foundation of healthier, more fulfilling relationships.

Consider Jane, who had just come out of a toxic relationship. She constantly blamed herself for the breakup and felt unworthy of love. Through self-love practices, she began to see her value and stopped seeking validation from others. She started journaling her thoughts and feelings, which helped her process her emotions. Over time, Jane noticed a significant decrease in her anxiety levels. She felt more confident and at peace with herself. This newfound self-love improved her mental health and attracted healthier relationships.

Another powerful testimonial comes from Sarah, who struggled with depression for years. She felt trapped in a cycle of negative self-talk and low self-esteem. After learning about self-compassion, she started incorporating it into her daily life. She practiced mindfulness and self-compassion exercises, allowing herself to feel her emotions without judgment. She also asked "Higher Power" for help to get out of the depression every day. By being kinder to herself, she could navigate life's challenges with more resilience and less emotional turmoil.

These stories illustrate that self-love is not just a lofty ideal but a practical and transformative practice. The profound emotional and psychological benefits offer a path to a healthier, more fulfilling life. By embracing self-love, you equip yourself with the tools to navigate life's ups and downs with grace and strength. The research and real-life examples presented here underscore the power of self-love in fostering emotional resilience, reducing stress, and enhancing overall well-being.

Mini Actions You Can Take: 1.2

Put this where you'll see it every morning, like on your bathroom mirror: "I am a unique masterpiece, perfectly crafted for this world. I lack nothing. I possess all the necessary abilities and skills to excel at tasks when given to me. Today, I will shine brightly and care for those around me."

1.3 COMMON MYTHS AND MISCONCEPTIONS ABOUT SELF-LOVE

One of the most pervasive myths about self-love is that it equates to narcissism or selfishness. It's easy to see why this misconception exists. Society often portrays self-love as vanity or self-centeredness. However, self-love is far from narcissism. Narcissism involves an inflated sense of self-importance and a lack of empathy for others.

In contrast, self-love is about having a balanced and realistic view of yourself. It's about recognizing your worth without diminishing the value of others. Self-love allows you to be kind to yourself without feeling superior to anyone else.

Another common misconception is that self-love is a privilege reserved for those with ample time and resources. The truth is that self-love is accessible to everyone, regardless of their circumstances. It's not about indulging in luxury but making choices that honor your well-being. You don't need to spend money on expensive spa treatments or vacations to practice self-love. Simple, everyday acts like setting aside time for yourself, saying no to things that drain you, and engaging in activities that bring you joy are potent forms of self-love. It's about finding small, meaningful ways to prioritize yourself daily.

There's also the belief that self-love means ignoring the needs of others. This couldn't be further from the truth. Self-love is a prerequisite for compassion towards others. When you care for yourself, you are better equipped to care for those around you. Think of it as filling your cup to pour into others without depleting yourself. Self-love helps you set boundaries, allowing you to be present and supportive of others without feeling overwhelmed or resentful. It's about creating a balance where your needs are met, enabling you to give from a place of abundance rather than scarcity.

Dr. Kristin Neff, a pioneering researcher in self-compassion, emphasizes that self-love is not about self-indulgence but self-respect. She explains that self-love involves treating yourself with the same kindness and understanding you would offer a close friend. This perspective shifts the focus from selfishness to self-care, highlighting that respecting your needs is crucial for overall well-being. Brené Brown, a renowned social researcher, echoes this sentiment. She says, "Owning our story and loving ourselves through that process is the bravest thing we will ever do." This quote underscores that self-love is about embracing who we are with all our imperfections.

To counter these myths practically, consider the example of setting boundaries. Many people fear that setting boundaries is selfish. However, boundaries are a form of self-love that protects your mental and emotional health. By clearly communicating your limits, you ensure your needs are respected, allowing you to interact more authentically and compassionately with others. For instance, if you need time alone to recharge after a long day, setting that boundary helps you show up more fully for your family later. This is not selfishness; it's self-preservation.

Another practical example is practicing self-compassion in everyday situations. Imagine you made a mistake at work. Instead of beating yourself up, you take a moment to recognize that everyone makes mistakes. You remind yourself that this doesn't define your worth. This act of self-compassion helps you learn from the experience without being paralyzed by self-criticism. It's a way of treating yourself with the same kindness you would extend to a friend who made an error. This improves your emotional resilience and enhances your performance and relationships at work.

In summary, debunking these myths is crucial for embracing self-love. Understanding that self-love is not narcissism, a privilege, or neglect of others' needs helps clear the path to genuine self-acceptance. By incorporating expert insights and practical examples, it becomes evident that self-love is a balanced, inclusive, and compassionate practice. It's about making choices that honor your well-being, setting boundaries to protect your mental health, and practicing self-compassion daily. This redefined view of self-love paves the way for a healthier, more fulfilling existence.

Mini Actions You Can Take: 1.3

When you fail, remember to separate yourself from the failure. Instead of thinking, "I'm a failure," view it as, "Today, I learned an important lesson."

1.4 THE CONNECTION BETWEEN SELF-LOVE AND MENTAL HEALTH

Self-love is a powerful protective mechanism against mental health challenges like anxiety and depression. By practicing self-love, you establish a mental buffer that mitigates negative thoughts and emotions, which are common precursors to anxiety and depression. This practice absorbs life's shocks and stresses, making them less impactful. It also nurtures a positive self-image and boosts resilience, allowing you to cope with life's challenges more effectively without feeling overwhelmed.

A significant benefit of self-love is its enhancement of your self-image. Viewing yourself with compassion and acceptance shifts your focus from perceived flaws to strengths and accomplishments. This positive perspective enhances your confidence and self-esteem, equipping you with the self-assurance needed to face the world and diminishes the adverse effects of social comparison and external criticism.

Moreover, self-love is a preventive measure against mental health issues by building resilience. Regular self-affirmation and recognizing your worth and capabilities fortify your mental and emotional defenses, making you less susceptible to stress and reducing the likelihood of anxiety and depression.

Mindfulness and self-compassion are other crucial aspects of self-love that help reduce stress. Mindfulness keeps you present and engaged, preventing preoccupation with past regrets or future worries. Self-compassion involves treating yourself kindly during tough times, lessening stress's emotional burden.

Consider Emily's story: She battled social anxiety, fearing others' judgments and often avoiding social interactions. By incorporating self-love practices like positive affirmations and deep breathing exercises before social events, Emily significantly improved her anxiety levels. She grew more confident and less concerned about others' opinions, transforming her social anxiety into a manageable part of her life.

Similarly, Lisa faced burnout from her demanding job, feeling mentally and physically exhausted. To rejuvenate, she prioritized self-love, dedicating time daily to enjoyable and relaxing activities and practicing mindfulness. These efforts significantly enhanced her energy and mental health, making her more resilient and capable of handling work pressures.

To integrate self-love into your mental health routine, start with a simple daily gratitude journal. Write down three things you are grateful for each day to shift your focus from deficiencies to abundance, promoting a positive mindset.

Mini Actions You Can Take: 1.4

1. When you start feeling sad about the past or worried about the future, concentrate on the present. Close your eyes and think about something that makes you feel peaceful,

positive, and joyful. If it's difficult, ask a 'Higher Power' for assistance.

2. Write down or think three things you appreciated today before bedtime

3. Write down one or two ways your strengths helped you or others today. For example, "My patience helped my son solve math problems independently."

1.5 SELF-LOVE VS. SELFISHNESS: UNDERSTANDING THE DIFFERENCE

Self-love and selfishness are often confused, yet they are entirely distinct concepts. Self-love is about self-respect and self-care. It's treating yourself with kindness, setting boundaries that protect your well-being, and nurturing your emotional, mental, and physical health. Self-love means recognizing your worth and taking steps to honor it. On the other hand, selfishness is characterized by the neglect of others' needs for personal gain. It's a selfish approach where one's actions are driven by self-interest without consideration for others. While self-love enriches your life and relationships, selfishness often harms them.

The societal stigma surrounding self-love stems from cultural norms that discourage self-prioritization. From a young age, many of us are taught to put others first, to be selfless, and to suppress our own needs for the sake of others. This mindset can lead to the misguided belief that any act of self-care is inherently selfish. Additionally, the fear of judgment from others can make it challenging to practice self-love openly. We worry about being labeled self-centered or vain when we take time for ourselves or set boundaries. This societal pressure can be a significant barrier to embracing self-love.

Consider a scenario where a woman is constantly inundated with unreasonable demands at work. If she says no to these demands to protect her mental health, she practices self-love. She recognizes that overextending herself will lead to burnout and compromise her well-being. This is a healthy boundary. In contrast, neglecting responsibilities, such as ignoring a friend's need for support during a crisis to pursue personal pleasure, would be selfish. The critical difference lies in the intent and impact of the actions. Self-love ensures that your needs are met without disregarding the needs of others, whereas selfishness prioritizes personal gain at the expense of others.

Another example can be found in social obligations. Imagine you have a family gathering to attend, but you're feeling emotionally drained and need some time alone to recharge. Choosing to prioritize your mental health by explaining your situation and opting out of the gathering is an act of self-love. It's about recognizing your limits and respecting them. In contrast, habitually avoiding social obligations with no regard for the feelings of others simply because you don't feel like attending can be considered selfish. The difference is that self-love involves a thoughtful consideration of your well-being and the well-being of others.

Practicing balanced self-love means setting healthy boundaries without guilt. It involves communicating your needs clearly and assertively, ensuring that your well-being is protected while maintaining respect for others. For instance, communicate this to your family if you need time to decompress after work. Let them know that this time helps you be more present and engaged with them. This way, you honor your need for self-care while considering your family's needs.

Empathy and compassion are integral to balanced self-love. Practicing self-love doesn't mean you disregard others; it means you include yourself in the circle of care. When you practice empathy and compassion, you can better understand and respect the needs of others while also honoring your own. For example, if a friend asks for help moving on a day you planned for self-care, you can express your willingness to help on another day. This approach shows empathy for your friend's needs while respecting your boundaries.

In summary, self-love and selfishness are fundamentally different. Self-love is about self-respect, self-care, and setting boundaries that honor your well-being. It's about balancing your needs with the needs of others, practicing empathy, and maintaining healthy relationships. Selfishness, in contrast, is driven by personal gain without regard for others. By understanding and embracing the difference, you can practice self-love in a way that enriches your life and those around you.

Mini Actions You Can Take: 1.5

Have the courage to say no: When faced with unreasonable demands at work or in personal relationships, it is essential to decline gently but firmly. Avoiding excessive burdens is crucial for protecting your mental and physical health.

Take time for self-evaluation: At the end of each day, reflect on your actions and emotions and be honest with yourself. This practice deepens self-understanding, helps you respect your values, and allows you to recognize areas needing improvement.

CHAPTER 2

OVERCOMING EMOTIONAL TRAUMA

I magine a young girl full of dreams, growing up in a family where her feelings are always overlooked. Whenever she expresses pain or sadness, she's told to "toughen up." Over time, these repeated dismissals build up, creating deep emotional wounds. As she becomes an adult, she often struggles in relationships and feels undeserving of love and respect. This narrative, or variations of it, is all too common for many women. Emotional trauma, if left unaddressed, can leave long-lasting scars. Recognizing and acknowledging these wounds is the first step toward healing.

2.1 THE IMPACT OF TOXIC RELATIONSHIPS ON SELF-ESTEEM

Toxic relationships can have a devastating effect on your self-esteem. When you're in a relationship where emotional manipulation is constant, it can warp your perception of yourself. You might start to believe you're inadequate, unworthy, or even responsible for the other person's behavior. Emotional manipulation often involves subtle tactics that make you question your reality and doubt your feelings. Over time, these manipulative behaviors can erode your self-worth, leaving you feeling powerless and confused. Gaslighting, a form of psychological manipulation where someone makes you doubt your sanity, further undermines self-esteem.

When you're constantly told that your feelings are irrational or that events didn't happen the way you remember, it can make you lose trust in your judgment and instincts.

Let's delve a bit deeper into gaslighting. Psychological gaslighting involves manipulating someone to doubt their memory, perception, and judgment. This term originated from the 1944 film "Gaslight," where the plot revolves around a husband who subtly alters the environment around his wife to make her doubt her sanity.

The techniques of gaslighting include the following features:

- **Denial of Information**: Denying the events or facts that the victim has experienced leads them to distrust their memory and perception.

- **Provision of False Information**: Providing lies or incorrect information makes it difficult for the victim to determine what is true.
- **Isolation of the Victim**: Severing the victim's relationships with friends and family, weakening their support system, and making the victim dependent on the perpetrator.
- **Destruction of the Victim's Self-Esteem**: Systematically diminishing the victim's self-esteem and confidence, thereby stripping them of the ability to make independent decisions and making them submissive.

Gaslighting can occur in domestic violence within the home, workplace harassment, and even in political contexts. Such behavior can have severe effects on the victim's mental health, making it crucial to recognize and address these issues.

Always maintain enough knowledge to view your situation objectively, have a support group you can consult, and keep a healthy mental state that allows you to assess situations and find solutions accurately.

Recognizing the signs of a toxic relationship is the first step toward reclaiming your self-worth. Constant criticism and belittling are major red flags. If someone frequently puts you down, mocks your achievements, or makes you feel small, it indicates a toxic dynamic. These behaviors chip away at your confidence, making you feel less capable and valuable.

Controlling behaviors and isolation are other common indicators. If your partner or friend tries to control your actions, decisions, or social interactions, it signifies an unhealthy relationship. Isolation tactics, like discouraging you from seeing friends or family, are designed to make you dependent on the toxic individual, further eroding your self-esteem.

Navigating and recovering from a toxic relationship requires strength and practical strategies.

Setting and enforcing personal boundaries is crucial. Clearly define what behaviors are unacceptable to you and communicate these boundaries assertively. For example, if constant criticism is an issue, let the person know that such remarks are hurtful and will no longer be tolerated. Enforcing boundaries might mean distancing yourself from the toxic individual if they refuse to respect your limits. Seeking support from trusted friends and family can provide the emotional backing you need. Surrounding yourself with people who genuinely care for you helps rebuild your self-esteem and offers a different perspective on your worth. They can remind you of your strengths and values, which are often overshadowed in toxic relationships.

Success stories can offer hope and inspiration. Consider Jessica, who was in a controlling relationship where her partner dictated her every move. She felt trapped and began believing she couldn't make decisions for herself. With the support of a close friend, Jessica mustered the courage to set boundaries. She communicated her need for independence and eventually decided to leave the relationship. Over time, Jessica regained her confidence and self-worth, realizing she was capable and strong.

Similarly, Emily endured years of emotional abuse that left her feeling worthless. She decided to seek therapy and leaned on her family for support. Through consistent effort and self-love practices, Emily rebuilt her self-esteem and formed healthier relationships.

Recovering self-worth after emotional abuse is a gradual process. It involves acknowledging the impact of the toxic relationship and taking deliberate steps to heal. One effective strategy is to engage in activities that make you feel good about yourself. Pursue hobbies or interests that you enjoy and excel in. These activities can serve as reminders of your capabilities and worth.

In summary, toxic relationships can severely damage your self-esteem, but recognizing the signs and taking proactive steps can help you reclaim your worth. Emotional manipulation, gaslighting, constant criticism, and controlling behaviors are all red flags that should not be ignored. Setting boundaries, seeking support, and engaging in self-love are essential recovery strategies. Remember, you deserve relationships that uplift and respect you. Your self-worth depends not on others' treatment of you, but on how you view and treat yourself.

Mini Actions You Can Take: 2.1

If you recognize harmful pressure, please seek support first. Talk to family, friends, school, or community counselors. You should never continue to endure it alone.

Imagine an "Angel Bubble." You are inside a bubble made of transparent, rubber-like material. Let's call this the "Angel Bubble." Suppose someone hurls meaningless insults at you, acts maliciously on purpose, or tries to corner you with some intention mentally. For simplicity, let's liken these negative actions to "throwing mud at you." This mud hits the transparent bubble and bounces back onto the person who threw it without touching you. You are merely observing this scene objectively. This "Angel Bubble" does exist. It is an invisible presence, a 'great force' that protects you with all its might.

This is also known as the "Law of the Mirror." When someone insults or belittles you, an invisible mirror exists between the speaker and you, and it is facing the speaker, reflecting their words to them, showing that their negativity says more about themselves than it does about you.

Conversely, if you encourage, praise, and express gratitude to someone, it is simultaneously directed at yourself. If you want others to treat you with compassion and respect, you must treat the people around you similarly. What you give will come back to you.

Do not receive the mud; do not throw the mud. It's pretty simple.

2.2 HEALING THE INNER CHILD: ADDRESSING CHILDHOOD TRAUMA

The concept of the inner child might seem abstract, but it holds significant weight in emotional health. Your inner child is the part of you that retains the feelings, memories, and experiences of your childhood. Addressing childhood trauma is vital for healing because these early experiences often shape your adult behavior, emotional responses, and self-esteem. When childhood wounds are left unattended, they manifest in various ways, affecting your ability to lead a fulfilling life.

Common childhood traumas include neglect, abandonment, and emotional abuse. Neglect occurs when a child's basic emotional needs are not met, leading to feelings of worthlessness and inadequacy. Abandonment, whether physical or emotional, leaves a void that can be difficult to fill. Emotional abuse, characterized by constant criticism, rejection, or manipulation, can severely damage a child's self-esteem. Witnessing domestic violence or experiencing bullying are also significant traumas. These experiences teach children that the world is unsafe and that they are powerless, carrying these beliefs into adulthood.

Consider visualizations to reconnect with and heal your inner child. These practices allow you to create a safe mental space to interact with your younger self. Imagine a peaceful place where you can meet your inner child. Visualize yourself comforting and reassuring them, letting them know they are loved and valued. This simple act can have a profound impact on your emotional well-being. Writing letters to your inner child is another effective technique. In these letters, they acknowledge the pain they experienced and offer the support and compassion they needed but didn't receive. Writing can be cathartic, helping you process and release long-held emotions.

Personal stories often illuminate the path to healing. Consider Emma, who grew up feeling neglected by emotionally unavailable parents. As an adult, she struggled with feelings of unworthiness and found it hard to form meaningful relationships. She visualized herself hugging her younger self, offering words of comfort and love. This practice helped Emma understand that her feelings of unworthiness were rooted in her childhood experiences, not her intrinsic value. Over time, she learned to nurture herself, improving her self-esteem and relationship skills.

Another example is Maya, who witnessed domestic violence throughout her childhood. The trauma left her feeling anxious and fearful, impacting her ability to trust others. Maya decided to write letters to her inner child, acknowledging the fear and confusion she felt during those violent episodes. She reassured her younger self that she was not to blame and that she deserved to feel safe and loved. This act of writing allowed Maya to release the pent-up emotions she had carried for years. It also helped her develop a sense of self-compassion, which was crucial for her healing process.

Healing the inner child is not a one-time event but an ongoing practice. Regularly engaging in activities that bring you joy and make you feel safe can help nurture your inner child. This might include hobbies you enjoyed as a child, spending time in nature, or simply allowing yourself to play and be creative. These activities remind your inner child that it's okay to feel joy and that they are in a safe and loving environment.

Mini Actions You Can Take: 2.2

Reconnecting with your inner child and addressing childhood trauma is an essential step towards healing. This process helps us understand the origins of our present struggles and opens the path to emotional liberation. Speak to your inner child, saying, "It was tough, but you made it through. That painful experience has now become a source of strength and light for you, all thanks to the 'Great Power.' This power chose you, trusting that you could endure this trial, and it gave you the inner strength to use your experiences to assist others who suffer as you did." Release a red balloon called 'Past You' into the sky, carrying love messages for others in pain. As the balloon vanishes from sight, recite the following: "As that balloon bursts somewhere above, may my countless messages of love reach those who need it, showing me that my painful past has been transformed into a tool to help others with love."

2.3 EMOTIONAL FREEDOM TECHNIQUES (EFT): PRACTICAL EXERCISES FOR HEALING

Emotional Freedom Techniques, commonly known as EFT or tapping, offer a powerful way to address and heal emotional distress. EFT combines elements of cognitive therapy with acupressure by tapping on specific meridian points on the body while focusing on a particular issue. This method can help reduce stress, anxiety, and even symptoms of post-traumatic stress disorder (PTSD). The basics of EFT involve identifying the emotional issue you want to address, whether it's a specific trauma, a phobia, or even a persistent negative thought. The process involves tapping nine particular points on the body while repeating affirmations related to the issue.

Basic Steps of EFT:

- Identifying the Issue: Before starting EFT, clearly identify the specific problem or emotion you want to address. This will be the focus of your session.
- Evaluating Intensity: Rate the issue's intensity from 0 to 10 on a scale. This will serve as a benchmark for assessing the session's effectiveness later.
- Preparing the Setup Statement: Acknowledge the problem and express self-acceptance with a setup statement. For example, "Even though I have this [problem], I deeply and completely accept myself." While saying this setup statement, lightly tap on the edge of the hand on the side of the pinky (the karate chop point).

- Tapping: Lightly tap on specific meridian points.
- The main tapping points are as follows:
  - Top of the head
  - Beginning of the eyebrows
  - Side of the eyes
  - Under the eyes
  - Under the nose
  - Under the chin
  - Below the collarbone
  - Under the arm (about 4 inches below the armpit)
- Tap each point 5 to 7 times while repeating a short phrase related to the issue.
- Reevaluation: After each round of tapping, reevaluate the intensity of the problem. Repeat the process if the intensity does not change or is still high.
- End the session when you feel a decrease in emotional intensity. Finally, take a deep breath and pay attention to the sensations in your body and mind.

Benefits of EFT:

- **Stress Reduction**: EFT has been shown to reduce stress hormones like cortisol.
- **Anxiety Relief**: It helps to lower anxiety levels, providing a tool for managing anxiety disorders.
- **Pain Management**: EFT can help reduce physical pain by altering brain pathways related to pain.
- **Aid for Depression**: It may improve depressive symptoms by tackling underlying emotional issues.

Considerations:

While EFT is gaining popularity and has been used effectively for various emotional and physical conditions, it is still considered controversial in some conventional medical circles. Critics argue that more rigorous, scientifically controlled studies are needed to validate their efficacy fully. Nonetheless, many individuals find it valuable to their wellness routines because it 2can be practiced independently after proper training.

It's always a good idea to consult with healthcare professionals before beginning any new therapy, especially for severe or chronic health issues.

The science behind EFT supports its effectiveness. According to a study published by the National Center for Biotechnology Information, EFT has been shown to reduce symptoms of anxiety, depression, and PTSD significantly. Participants in the study experienced a 40% reduction in anxiety, a 35% decrease in depression, and a 32% reduction in PTSD symptoms after a four-day EFT workshop.

The theory behind EFT is that tapping on specific meridian points helps to balance the body's energy system. This balance can reduce the emotional impact of memories and stressors, leading to a more relaxed and positive emotional state. The connection between EFT and energy meridians is similar to principles found in traditional Chinese medicine, which uses acupressure and acupuncture to treat various ailments by balancing the body's energy flow.

Consider the story of Anna, who struggled with anxiety for years. Traditional therapy provided some relief, but her anxiety would often resurface during stressful situations. A friend recommended EFT, and Anna decided to give it a try. She started tapping on the points while focusing on her anxiety about public speaking. After several sessions, Anna noticed that her anxiety levels decreased significantly. She felt more confident and less fearful when speaking in front of others. EFT became a regular part of her self-care routine, helping her manage anxiety more effectively.

Another powerful example is Mia, who experienced a traumatic event during her childhood. This trauma haunted her for years, affecting her relationships and overall well-being. Mia attended an EFT workshop where she learned to tap on specific points while focusing on her traumatic memory. Through consistent practice, she felt the emotional charge of the memory diminish. Mia found that EFT not only helped her process the trauma but also empowered her to move forward with a sense of peace and resilience.

EFT offers a practical and accessible way to address emotional wounds and promote healing. By combining cognitive therapy with the physical act of tapping on meridian points, EFT provides a holistic approach to emotional well-being. The step-by-step process is simple to follow and can be done anywhere, making it a valuable tool for managing stress, anxiety, and trauma. The success stories of individuals like Anna and Mia demonstrate the transformative potential of EFT. Whether you're dealing with a specific trauma or seeking to improve your overall emotional health, EFT can be a powerful addition to your self-care toolkit.

Mini Actions You Can Take: 2.3

Lie on your bed, dim the lights, relax, take four slow, deep breaths, and start practicing EFT. By the end of the session, your mind should feel more apparent, and your mood should be lighter and more joyful.

2.4 BUILDING RESILIENCE: OVERCOMING EMOTIONAL SETBACKS

Resilience is the ability to bounce back from adversity and emotional setbacks. It allows you to remain strong and move forward despite life's challenges. Resilient individuals adapt well to adversity, trauma, or significant stress. They possess a combination of mental toughness and emotional flexibility, enabling them to recover from setbacks and continue pursuing their goals. Resilience plays a crucial role in emotional recovery by providing the strength needed to navigate through difficult times and emerge stronger on the other side.

One characteristic of resilient individuals is their ability to maintain a positive outlook, even in challenging situations. They focus on what they can control and let go of what they cannot. This mindset helps them stay grounded and hopeful, reducing the emotional toll of setbacks. Another key trait is emotional regulation. Resilient people can manage their emotions effectively, preventing negative feelings from overwhelming them. They use coping strategies to deal with stress and seek support when needed. Resilience also involves a sense of purpose and meaning, which motivates during challenging times. These characteristics collectively contribute to emotional healing and recovery.

Building resilience is gradual, but practical methods exist to strengthen it. Cultivating a positive mindset is a foundational step.

When we experience a significant disaster or feel overwhelmed by dark emotions, our human hearts can sometimes retreat into a well of shock. It's a narrow, dark place, cut off from society. We can look up and see the blue sky and hear children's laughter, but we can't find a way out of the well. Retreating into this shell is a state that makes us more vulnerable to depression.

At times like this, the first thing you need to do is stay connected with others. Talk to family and friends—it's better to have two people than one, and a few people are better than two. Contact local support groups and ask at your local library or church. Do not stay alone. If possible, talk to someone every day.

Next, try to understand your situation objectively. Assess what has happened to you and consider how it has impacted your physical, mental, and financial health. Try to identify the options you have for navigating these challenges. If you still need to feel ready to think through these options, keep talking to others until you do. Over time, you will begin to feel like yourself again.

Finally, act. Don't just focus on what you've lost or lack. All of us have been given our own set of cards to play in life. List everything you have: You can see, you can hear, you can walk, you can read and write, you can use a computer, you have family and friends you can talk to, and you may even have some money. Be grateful for all these things and use each card fully. Lay out all your choices for moving forward and pick one path to follow. There's no need to worry—like a ship, you can change course anytime. There is no such thing as a "wrong path."

You can constantly adjust your direction if something doesn't go as planned. Whatever path you choose will have a mix of positives and negatives. In life, there is no "best path." All we can do is give our best as we journey forward. An incredible force will guide you along the way. When you face situations that make you hesitate, this greater force will lead you, helping you find the right words and actions. If you strongly desire something, you will be guided toward it.

So, don't hesitate. An incredible force is with you. Walk forward proudly, stand tall, and smile as you go.

Stress management techniques are vital for building resilience. Identify your stressors and develop healthy coping mechanisms. Physical activities such as exercise or walking can release endorphins, which boost your mood and help you handle stress better. Engaging in hobbies or activities you enjoy can also provide a mental break and reduce stress levels. Additionally, maintaining a support network is crucial. Surround yourself with positive, supportive people who uplift and encourage you. Social connections provide emotional support and can be a source of strength during tough times.

Self-compassion is a cornerstone of resilience. Being kind to yourself during difficult times can significantly aid emotional recovery. Self-compassion involves treating yourself with the same kindness and understanding that you would offer a friend. It means recognizing that everyone makes mistakes and experiences setbacks. This perspective reduces self-blame and fosters a more positive self-view. Self-compassionate self-talk is particularly beneficial. When faced with a setback, try saying, "It's okay to feel this way instead of criticizing yourself. I'm doing my best, and I will get through this." This shift in self-talk can mitigate the emotional impact of setbacks and promote healing.

Consider the story of Laura, who faced a major setback when she unexpectedly lost her job. Initially, she felt overwhelmed and doubted her abilities. However, Laura decided to focus on building resilience. She cultivated a positive mindset by listing her strengths and past achievements. She practiced mindfulness daily; instead of being filled with anxiety about what would happen after losing her job, she focused on the 'now'—the 'now' of job hunting and the 'now' of cooking. That helped her stay calm and focused. Laura also relied on her support network, seeking encouragement from friends and family. Through self-compassionate self-talk, she reminded herself that losing a job did not reflect her worth. Over time, Laura found a new job that aligned better with her skills and passion, showcasing the power of resilience.

Another example is Maria, who experienced a significant loss when she lost a loved one. The grief was overwhelming, but Maria knew she needed to build resilience to cope. She thought about people who lived while bearing even greater sorrow than herself. For example, consider a woman who lost her husband and three young children in a car accident or a five-year-old boy who lost his parents, grandparents, and all his siblings in a natural disaster and was subsequently placed in an orphanage. She drew courage from people in such circumstances; through this, she could stand up repeatedly, determined to live on with strength.   Maria also engaged in activities that brought her joy, helping her find moments of happiness amid the grief. She practiced self-compassion, allowing herself to feel the pain without judgment. This approach helped Maria navigate through her grief, eventually finding a sense of peace and acceptance.

Mini Actions You Can Take: 2.4

You have two options for handling past traumas. The first option is to believe, "I was treated this way and endured such painful experiences, which have defined who I am Today. Nothing, not even I, can change that." The second option is to think, "I was treated this way and went through these painful experiences, but I will use them as fertilizer. Because of these experiences, I can be more compassionate towards others, offer encouragement to those who have suffered similarly, and strengthen myself to overcome future challenges. I have gained an inner strength that only comes from overcoming suffering." The choice is yours. Please choose one and declare, "I choose this one."

2.5 THE ROLE OF THERAPY AND COUNSELING IN HEALING

Therapy and counseling offer invaluable support in the healing process. Talking to a professional can provide a safe space to explore your emotions and experiences without judgment. Therapists are trained to help you understand and navigate your feelings, offering tools and strategies to cope with trauma and emotional distress. Various types of therapy are available, each with its unique approach. Cognitive Behavioral Therapy (CBT) focuses on identifying and changing negative thought patterns. Dialectical Behavior Therapy (DBT) combines cognitive-behavioral techniques with mindfulness. Trauma-focused therapies, such as Eye Movement Desensitization and Reprocessing (EMDR), specifically address traumatic experiences. Therapy aims to help you develop healthier coping mechanisms and improve your emotional well-being.

Selecting the right therapist is crucial for effective healing. Start by considering the therapist's specialization and approach. If you're dealing with trauma, a therapist trained in trauma-focused therapies would be beneficial. Ask potential therapists about their experience with issues similar to yours. Inquire about their therapeutic approach and how they plan to help you achieve your goals. It's also important to consider the therapist's personality and communication style. You should feel comfortable and understood during your sessions. Trust your instincts; if something doesn't feel right, looking for another therapist is okay. Therapy is a personal experience, and finding the right fit can significantly affect your healing journey.

Many people hesitate to seek therapy due to common misconceptions and fears. One prevalent misconception is that treatment is only for "severe" issues. In reality, therapy can benefit anyone, regardless of the intensity of their struggles. Whether you're dealing with everyday stress or deep-seated trauma, therapy provides tools and support to improve your mental health. Another fear is the potential for judgment. It's natural to worry about opening up to a stranger, but therapists are trained to create a non-judgmental, supportive environment. Their role is to help you, not to judge or criticize. Remember, seeking help is a sign of strength, not weakness. It's an acknowledgment that you deserve support and healing.

Group therapy can also be incredibly transformative. Consider the story of Jessica, who felt isolated and alone in her struggles with anxiety. She decided to join a group therapy session, hoping to find support and understanding. In the group, Jessica met others who shared similar experiences. This sense of community helped her realize she was not alone in her struggles. The group provided a supportive environment where she could express her feelings openly. The collective wisdom and encouragement from group members played a significant role in her healing process. Jessica found strength in knowing that others were on a similar path, and this connection helped her build resilience and confidence.

Therapy and counseling offer a structured, supportive approach to healing. By providing a safe space to explore your emotions, therapy helps you understand and process your experiences. Finding the right therapist, addressing common fears, and learning from success stories can guide you toward effective healing. Whether through individual or group therapy, professional support can be a powerful catalyst for emotional well-being. As you seek help, remember that you are taking an important step toward self-love and recovery, paving the way for a healthier, more fulfilling life.

Finding a counselor or therapist is a great step toward mental well-being, and there are several ways to find the right one for you. Here's a guide to help you find a therapist and understand potential costs:

How to Find a Counselor or Therapist

1. **Check with Your Insurance Provider:** Your provider may cover some or all therapy costs if you have health insurance. Check your insurance's mental health coverage, as it often has a list of approved therapists within its network, which can reduce costs significantly.
2. **Ask for Recommendations:** Ask a trusted friend, family member, or healthcare provider for recommendations, especially if they have had positive experiences. Word of mouth can help you find local counselors with good reputations.
3. **Community Mental Health Centers:** Many communities have mental health centers or organizations that offer therapy services on a sliding scale based on income, or sometimes even for free. Libraries, community centers, and local government websites often have this information.
4. **University Counseling Services:** If you're a student, universities and colleges often offer counseling services at reduced rates or for free. Additionally, some universities have clinics where graduate psychology students provide therapy under supervision, often at lower costs.

Therapy Fees: What to Expect

1. Typical Costs

Therapy costs vary widely depending on where you live, the therapist's qualifications, and whether they accept insurance. In the U.S., for example, standard sessions can range from $75 to $200 per session. In larger cities, fees can be higher.

2. Insurance Coverage

Insurance may cover some or all therapy costs if mental health services are included in your plan. You'll generally pay less if you choose an in-network therapist.

3. Sliding Scale Fees

Some therapists offer sliding scale fees, meaning the cost adjusts based on your income. Don't hesitate to ask a therapist if they offer this option—many do.

4. Low-Cost or Free Options

Community health centers, university clinics, and nonprofit organizations often offer affordable therapy. Some religious or spiritual organizations also provide counseling at reduced rates or even free.

If you're on a tight budget, start with sliding scale options, community mental health centers, or teletherapy platforms. Many resources are available to make therapy accessible and affordable.

Mini Actions You Can Take: 2.5

If necessary, discuss the situation with family or friends and then use the methods described above to contact a counselor.

In the next chapter, we will explore practical steps to silence your inner critic and build a foundation of self-love. This journey will equip you with tools to challenge negative self-talk and foster a supportive inner dialogue.

CHAPTER 3

SILENCING THE INNER CRITIC

I magine a young girl, full of dreams and eager to take on the world. She's curious, vibrant, and unafraid to speak her mind. But slowly, voices from her surroundings start to chip away at her confidence. A parent's harsh words, a teacher's dismissive comment, or a peer's cruel joke—all these moments collect like pebbles in her heart. Over time, these external voices turn inward, becoming her critical inner voice. This inner critic, born from the echoes of her past, shadows her every move, questioning her worth and abilities. If this resonates with you, know that you are not alone. Understanding the origins and impacts of this inner critic is the first step to silence it.

3.1 UNDERSTANDING YOUR INNER CRITIC: ORIGINS AND IMPACTS

The origins of the inner critic are deeply rooted in our childhood experiences. When children grow up feeling that they are never considered good enough, they internalize a sense of being flawed. Parental influence plays a significant role here. Parents who are overly critical, controlling, or indifferent can inadvertently implant a harsh inner critic in their child. This internal voice, shaped by the quest for parental approval, becomes an automatic coping mechanism. It starts to navigate childhood difficulties but persists into adulthood, continuing to judge and criticize.

Societal pressures and cultural norms further nurture this inner critic. From a young age, we are bombarded with messages about how we should look, behave, and achieve. These societal expectations set rigid and often unrealistic standards, making it easy to feel inadequate. The media amplifies these pressures by portraying perfect lives and flawless appearances. Cultural norms prioritizing success and perfection over well-being can make self-compassion seem like a weakness. These external pressures shape our inner dialogue, making it a relentless critic that constantly measures us against impossible ideals.

Major life events and traumatic experiences also contribute to the development of the inner critic. Traumatic events, such as abuse, significant loss, or failure, can leave deep emotional scars. These experiences often lead to a heightened sense of self-doubt and a fear of repeating past mistakes. The inner critic acts as a misguided protector, trying to prevent further pain by harshly reminding us of our perceived flaws and failures. Though its intention may be protective, its impact is overwhelmingly negative, perpetuating feelings of inadequacy and unworthiness.

The impact of the inner critic on self-esteem is profound. Constant self-doubt and second-guessing erode self-worth and confidence. This relentless internal dialogue makes it difficult to trust your judgment, leading to a perpetual state of uncertainty. Increased anxiety and stress levels are expected consequences of a dominant inner critic. The fear of making mistakes or failing can be paralyzing, preventing you from taking risks or pursuing your goals. This hesitation stifles personal growth and reinforces a cycle of underachievement and low self-esteem.

Common themes of the inner critic include criticizing your appearance or abilities, undermining your achievements, and fearing failure or rejection. For instance, you might look in the mirror and immediately focus on perceived flaws, ignoring your unique beauty. Or you might achieve something significant, only to downplay your success with thoughts like, "It wasn't that big of a deal" or "Anyone could have done it." This inner dialogue keeps you trapped in a cycle of self-criticism and doubt.

Reflection Exercise on Identifying the Themes of Your Inner Critic

Take a moment to reflect on the general themes of your inner critic. Ask yourself the following questions and jot down your thoughts:

- What are the repetitive negative thoughts you have about your appearance or abilities?
- How do you typically undermine your achievements?
- In what situations do you fear failure or rejection the most?

Recognizing these patterns is the first step toward challenging and changing them. Understanding the origins and impacts of your inner critic is crucial for freeing yourself from its control. By recognizing where these critical voices come from, you can start to see them for what they are—misguided attempts to protect you. This awareness will help you build a foundation for a healthier, more supportive inner dialogue.

Let's deepen your self-reflection on your inner critic using the following action examples. By working on each step, you can recognize the critical voices within and take a step towards fostering a more positive self-dialogue:

1. Recognize Repetitive Negative Thoughts
   ◦ Example: "I often think, 'I am less attractive or capable than others,' which makes me feel inferior. When such negative thoughts arise, I'll remind myself not to compare myself to others. If I do compare, I'll compare my current self to where I was six months ago to recognize my growth."
2. Recognize Patterns of Undermining Your Achievements
   ◦ Example: "I tend to dismiss my achievements thinking, 'Anyone could do this; it's nothing special.' When I notice this habit, I'll write down each effort and accomplishment and reassess their value. If I need to measure my progress, I'll create my benchmarks. What skills do I have now that I didn't have a year ago? I'll reflect on my growth every six months, share it with family and friends, and celebrate small victories by dining out, enjoying my favorite cake at a cafe, or treating myself to a new accessory."
3. Identify Situations Where You Fear Failure or Rejection
   ◦ Example: "I especially fear failure or rejection when trying something new, like a job task or a hobby skill. I worry too much about others' perceptions if I fail. Before taking on a challenge, I'll focus on what I can learn and grow from it,

viewing it as a positive experience rather than fearing the outcome. A technique to reduce fear is to make the fear tangible by planning for failures and rejections, such as 'If I fail here, this is what I'll do.' 'If I'm rejected, I'll handle it this way.' For instance, if I'm worried about forgetting what to say during a presentation, I'll write the main points on paper and check them off as I go along. If I get stuck, I'll look at the paper and know what to discuss next."

Recognizing the themes and patterns of your inner critic through this reflection exercise can be the first step toward establishing a more supportive inner dialogue.

Mini Actions You Can Take: 3.1

Fear often comes from what we don't know. To tackle this, make fear more manageable by preparing for potential failures or rejections. For example, if you're concerned about forgetting your lines during a presentation, write down the key points and tick them off as you cover each one. If you lose your place, you can quickly refer back to your notes to find it. This kind of preparation helps you overcome fear and face challenges with a clearer mind.

3.2 TECHNIQUES TO QUIET NEGATIVE SELF-TALK

Practicing mindfulness is a powerful way to manage negative thoughts. When you practice mindfulness, you bring your attention to the present moment. This can help you become more aware of your negative self-talk and how it affects you. Mindfulness is a simple practice that involves sitting quietly, focusing on your breath, and keeping your mind clear. You can imagine the sky or ocean if it helps you clear your mind. When your mind wanders, gently bring your focus back to your breathing. Over time, this practice helps you become more aware of your thoughts without getting caught up in them. It creates a space between you and your inner critic, allowing you to observe your thoughts without judgment.

Beyond mindfulness, one way to deal with persistent negative thoughts is to think about something enjoyable instead. For instance, if painful memories from the past start to haunt you, consider what you'll eat for dinner, plan who you'll meet over the weekend, or think about what you'd like to do during your time after dinner. By replacing thoughts that cause you distress with thoughts that entertain you, you naturally stop dwelling on the negative ones. It may not be easy to switch your focus right away, but as you make it a habit, you'll notice a decrease in the frequency of being dominated by negative thoughts after a week or two.

Let's imagine someone gave a 5-year-old girl a sharp knife. She knows it's dangerous and could hurt her, but she doesn't know what to do with it. Then, you take the knife from her hands and give her a cute stuffed animal instead. Suddenly, the girl smiles. Would you continue holding onto something that could hurt you, or would you replace it with something that makes you smile?

Another technique involves using visualizations. Imagine a stop sign each time a negative thought comes to mind. This mental image can be a powerful reminder to halt negative self-talk. You can also imagine a remote control and visualize switching the channel to your favorite music or cooking show when negative thoughts appear. These visual cues can help you disrupt the flow of negativity and regain control of your thoughts.

Encouraging positive self-talk is not just a suggestion; it's a crucial step in your journey to self-improvement. It's about replacing negative thoughts with affirming statements. Start by creating a list of positive affirmations that resonate with you. These might include phrases like "I am capable and strong," "I deserve happiness," or "I am worthy of love and respect." Practice positive self-talk daily by repeating these affirmations each morning or whenever you think negatively. Over time, these positive statements can rewire your brain, making adopting a more positive outlook more accessible. Writing these affirmations in a journal can also reinforce their impact. You solidify their presence in your mind each time you write them down.

Grounding exercises are another effective way to stay present and reduce anxiety. The 5-4-3-2-1 grounding technique is a simple yet powerful exercise. Start by identifying five things you can see around you. Next, focus on four things you can touch, followed by three things you can hear. Then, notice two things you can smell and one can taste. This exercise engages your senses and brings your attention back to the present moment, helping to ground you and reduce anxious thoughts.

Deep breathing exercises can also be incredibly calming. Try inhaling deeply through your nose for a count of four, holding your breath for four counts, and then exhaling slowly through your mouth for a count of four. Repeat this several times to help calm your mind and body.

Journaling Prompt: Transforming Negative Self-Talk

Take a moment to reflect on your negative self-talk. Write down some common negative thoughts you experience. Then, write a positive affirmation for each negative thought that counteracts it. For example, if you often think, "I can't do this," replace it with, "I am capable of overcoming challenges." Practice using these affirmations whenever negative thoughts arise.

Incorporating these techniques into your daily routine can significantly reduce the power of your inner critic.

By practicing focusing on the present, using thought-stopping techniques, encouraging positive self-talk, and engaging in grounding exercises, you create a toolkit that helps you manage and quiet negative self-talk. These practices help you become more aware of your thoughts and empower you to change them, fostering a more positive and compassionate relationship with yourself.

Mini Actions You Can Take: 3.2

When negative thoughts don't leave your mind, imagine changing the channel on a TV remote. Display images you enjoy on the new channel based on your current mood. It could be a forest with a stream's murmur and birds' sound. Maybe you are lying on the grass under a blue sky, watching birds fly overhead while taking deep breaths. Is a close friend beside you? Whether it's a music show, a cooking show, or a travel program, imagine a channel that calms and entertains you according to your mood. Then, with a smile, say, "I choose to enjoy today."

3.3 REFRAMING NEGATIVE THOUGHTS: COGNITIVE RESTRUCTURING

Cognitive restructuring is a powerful technique for changing negative thought patterns. It's about identifying and challenging the distortions in your thinking that lead to negative emotions. These distortions are often automatic and go unnoticed, but they can profoundly impact your self-esteem and overall well-being. The goal of cognitive restructuring is to shift those negative thoughts to more balanced and realistic perspectives. By doing this, you can reduce the emotional pain associated with these thoughts and improve your mental health.

One of the first steps in cognitive restructuring is identifying cognitive distortions. These distortions are flawed ways of thinking that can lead to negative emotions. Common distortions include all-or-nothing thinking, where you see things in black and white with no middle ground. Another is overgeneralization, where you see a single adverse event as a never-ending pattern of defeat. Catastrophizing is another distortion where you expect the worst possible outcome. By recognizing these patterns, you can challenge them and change your thinking.

Once you've identified the distortions, the next step is to challenge and reframe these negative thoughts. This involves questioning the validity of your thoughts and considering alternative perspectives. Ask yourself if there's evidence to support your negative thoughts or if you're jumping to conclusions. Consider whether you're focusing only on the negatives and ignoring any positives. By challenging these thoughts, you can begin to see them in a more balanced light. For instance, if you think, "I'm a total failure because I made a mistake," challenge this by asking, "Is it true that one mistake makes me a total failure? What about all the things I've done right?"

The ABC model, developed by Dr. Albert Ellis, is a practical framework for cognitive restructuring. It stands for Activating event, Belief, and Consequence. Start by identifying the activating event, which is the situation that triggered your negative thoughts. Next, identify the belief, which is your interpretation of the event. Finally, the consequence, the emotional and behavioral response to the belief, is determined. The key to changing your thought patterns lies in disputing irrational beliefs. Ask yourself if the belief is based on facts or assumptions. Consider alternative explanations and how you might view the situation differently. By doing this, you can change the emotional and behavioral consequences.

Let's give two simple examples.

Example 1:

- Activating Event (A): Your idea is rejected during a meeting.
- Belief (B): "My opinions are worthless."
- Consequence (C): You feel down and hesitate to share your opinions in future meetings.

To counter this belief (B), you could encourage yourself by thinking, "It was just this idea that wasn't the right fit, not that all my ideas are unacceptable," or you could take the approach of asking for specific feedback to identify improvements. This can help you regain confidence and participate actively again.

Example 2:

- Activating Event (A): You receive critical comments from a parent.
- Belief (B): "I am not acknowledged by my parents."
- Consequence (C): Your self-esteem is hurt, and you feel sad.

In this case, you could reinterpret the belief (B) as "My parents are not perfect either, and it might be their way of expressing love." Additionally, taking action by asking specifically what was problematic can help clear up misunderstandings and potentially build a more constructive relationship. This can help you overcome sadness and improve the parent-child relationship.

These examples illustrate how challenging negative automatic thoughts and adopting a more realistic and optimistic perspective can change emotional and behavioral responses to be more positive.

Keeping a thought journal is an effective exercise for practicing cognitive restructuring. Daily, write down the negative thoughts that come to mind, the activating event, and your emotional response. Then, use the ABC model to analyze these thoughts and challenge distortions. Write alternative, more balanced thoughts and note how this changes your emotional response. Over time, this practice can help you develop a habit of challenging negative thoughts and replacing them with more positive ones.

Another practical exercise is writing alternative, positive thoughts. Whenever you catch yourself thinking negatively, take a moment to write down a more positive or realistic thought. For example, if you think, "I can't do anything right," write down, "I make mistakes, but I also do many things well." This simple act can help shift your mindset and reduce the impact of negative thoughts. The more you practice, the easier it will become to reframe your thoughts automatically.

Consider the story of Alice, who struggled with imposter syndrome. Impostor Syndrome refers to a psychological state in which, despite achieving success and accomplishments, one feels that this success is not due to their own abilities or achievements, but rather due to external factors such as luck, misunderstandings by others, or timing. People suffering from this syndrome often feel like they are 'frauds' and fear that their 'true' incompetence will eventually be exposed to others.

This condition is particularly prominent in the workplace or academic settings and is often more acutely felt in environments where high achievements are expected. Those with Impostor Syndrome find it difficult to objectively evaluate their success and tend to have extremely low self-esteem.

As a coping mechanism, it is important to acknowledge that one's success is not merely due to chance or external factors, but also due to their own efforts and abilities, thereby boosting self-esteem. Additionally, sharing emotions with a trusted individual can help bridge the gap between one's perceptions and reality, making it easier to understand.

Despite her accomplishments, Alice constantly felt like a fraud at work. Through cognitive restructuring, she identified her cognitive distortions and began challenging them. She realized she was over-generalizing her mistakes and ignoring her successes. By using the ABC model and keeping a thought journal, Alice was able to reframe her negative thoughts. She started to see herself as competent and capable, which reduced her feelings of self-doubt.

Another example is Rachel, who had a habit of negative self-perception. She often thought she was unattractive and unworthy of love. By practicing cognitive restructuring, Rachel identified her distortions and challenged them. She realized she focused only on her perceived flaws and ignored her positive qualities. By writing alternative, positive thoughts, Rachel began to see herself in a more balanced light. This shift in perception improved her self-esteem and made her feel more confident in her relationships.

Mini Actions You Can Take: 3.3

Let's list some things that make you feel pessimistic about yourself and try to rephrase them positively.

For example, "I often think about my introverted personality as a lack of sociability and inability to express my thoughts clearly in front of others. However, from now on, I will think: 'I cherish my alone time, as it is the source of my creativity and concentration.' 'I think deeply, allowing me to provide higher quality ideas and solutions.' 'My listening skills lay the foundation for building deep relationships with others.' 'My quietness brings peace and calm, giving those around me a sense of security.'"

Standing straight with your chest out and constantly smiling will instill confidence and ease in your mind.

3.4 DEVELOPING A GROWTH MINDSET: EMBRACING IMPERFECTION

The concept of a growth mindset, introduced by psychologist Carol Dweck, revolves around the belief that abilities and intelligence can be developed through dedication and hard work. This contrasts with a fixed mindset, where people believe their talents and intelligence are static and unchangeable. Embracing a growth mindset is crucial for self-improvement because it encourages you to see challenges as learning opportunities rather than insurmountable obstacles. When you adopt this mindset, you open yourself to the benefits of pushing beyond your comfort zone and learning from your experiences, including your mistakes.

One key strategy for developing a growth mindset is to reframe how you view challenges. Instead of seeing them as threats to your competence, consider their opportunities to grow and improve. Remember that every expert was once a beginner when encountering a difficult task. Embrace the learning process and celebrate your efforts, regardless of the immediate outcome. This shift in perspective can make daunting tasks seem more manageable and exciting.

Viewing failures as learning experiences is another vital aspect of a growth mindset. Everyone fails at some point, but how you respond to failure matters. Instead of seeing failure as a reflection of your inadequacy, view it as a steppingstone to success. Analyze what went wrong, understand why it happened, and think about what you can do differently next time. This approach helps you learn from your mistakes and builds resilience, making it easier to bounce back from setbacks.

Consider the story of Lisa, who decided to learn a new skill—coding. Initially, she struggled with the technical jargon and complex problems. Her fixed mindset told her she wasn't cut out for it, but she adopted a growth mindset. She started viewing each mistake as a lesson and each setback as a chance to improve. Over time, her persistence paid off. She became proficient in coding and developed a newfound confidence in her ability to tackle new challenges.

Another example is Monica, who faced a significant career setback when she was passed over for a promotion. Initially, she felt defeated and questioned her abilities. However, by embracing a growth mindset, she reframed the experience. She saw it as an opportunity to develop new skills and improve her performance. Monica sought feedback, took additional training, and worked on her weaknesses. Her efforts were recognized, and she eventually earned the promotion, realizing that the setback had catalyzed personal and professional growth.

Self-compassion plays a crucial role in developing a growth mindset. Being kind to yourself is important, especially when things are unplanned. Practicing self-forgiveness allows you to move past your mistakes without being weighed down by guilt or regret. Remember that everyone makes mistakes; each is an opportunity to learn and grow. Instead of criticizing yourself for not being perfect, acknowledge your efforts and the progress you've made.

Celebrating small progress and achievements is another way to foster a growth mindset. Each step forward, no matter how small, is a victory worth acknowledging. This practice keeps you motivated and reinforces the belief that you can grow and improve. For instance, if you're working on a long-term project, take a moment to celebrate each milestone. These celebrations don't have to be grand; even a small reward or a moment of self-praise can make a significant difference.

Incorporating these strategies into your daily life can transform how you approach challenges and setbacks. By embracing a growth mindset, you improve your skills and abilities and cultivate a resilient and positive outlook. This mindset empowers you to face difficulties confidently, knowing that each experience, whether a success or a failure, is a valuable part of your personal growth.

Mini Actions You Can Take: 3.4

Remind yourself: "Growth and achieving goals take time. The most important things are persistence and not giving up."

3.5 SELF-COMPASSION PRACTICES: BEING GENTLE WITH YOURSELF

Self-compassion is about treating yourself with the kindness and understanding you would offer a dear friend. It involves recognizing your suffering, offering kindness, and understanding that suffering is a shared human experience. When it comes to silencing the inner critic, self-compassion is a powerful tool. It helps you respond to your inner critic with gentleness instead of harshness.

The three main components of self-compassion are self-kindness, common humanity, and mindfulness.

- Self-kindness involves being warm and understanding toward yourself when you suffer, fail, or feel inadequate, rather than ignoring your pain or flagellating yourself with self-criticism.

- Common humanity recognizes that suffering and personal inadequacy are part of the shared human experience—something we all go through rather than something that happens to "me" alone.
- Mindfulness involves being aware of your present moment experience without judgment, allowing you to observe your thoughts and feelings without being overwhelmed.

Individuals who practice self-compassion are more likely to:

- Display strength and resilience during difficult times
- Show forgiveness and empathy towards others
- Emphasize learning and personal development
- Feel genuine and build deep connections, fostering intimacy in relationships
- Demonstrate perseverance, motivation, and focus on achieving significant goals
- Establish clear boundaries and comfortably decline requests
- Manage workplace challenges effectively, feeling capable and competent
- Experience happiness, optimism, and life satisfaction
- Achieve a healthy balance between work and personal life
- Appreciate and feel content with their physical appearance
- Be responsible and conscientious about your actions
- Find compromise in conflicts
- Prioritize eating healthily and exercising
- Enjoy good quality sleep and maintain a robust immune system
- Possess a steady and unconditional self-esteem

If any of the above characteristics do not reflect your current experience, let's explore them together in small, manageable steps throughout this book.

The impact of self-compassion on emotional well-being is profound. By practicing self-compassion, you can reduce feelings of anxiety and depression. It fosters a sense of inner peace and acceptance, allowing you to navigate life's challenges with greater resilience. When you are compassionate toward yourself, you create a supportive internal environment that counteracts the negativity of the inner critic. This shift can lead to increased self-esteem and a more positive outlook on life.

One practical exercise for cultivating self-compassion is writing a compassionate letter to yourself. Think of a situation that made you feel inadequate or caused you suffering. Write a letter to yourself from the perspective of an empathetic friend. Offer understanding, kindness, and encouragement. This exercise can help you reframe your thoughts and foster a more compassionate inner dialogue.

Another practical technique for enhancing self-compassion is the emotion labeling method.

Emotion Labeling: Expressing emotions in specific words can help improve self-empathy. By describing complex or subtle emotional changes with particular words like "sad," "angry," or "confused," it is possible to objectively capture those emotions, which promotes understanding and acceptance of one's feelings. This process allows for proper self-response without being overwhelmed by emotions.

Let's look at the emotion labeling practice Sara performed and its results. Recently, Sara started living with her aunt, uncle, and their two children. She strives to adapt to the new environment, but the lack of privacy troubles her. In particular, the constant presence of family members means she cannot have time alone, making it difficult to maintain mental balance.

Step 1: Emotion Labeling

One day, Sara retreated to her room to organize her emotions by writing them down in a notebook. She wrote down "frustrated," "feeling isolated," and "feeling oppressed" and considered the specific situations each emotion arose from.

- **Frustrated**: There is always someone around, so she has no space.
- **Feeling isolated**: She feels alone in dealing with her emotions, as others do not understand them.
- **Feeling oppressed**: Her routine is overwhelmed by her family's schedule.

Step 2: Deepening Understanding through Self-Dialogue

2Sara asked herself, "Why do I feel so uncomfortable?" Through self-dialogue, she re-realized how important privacy is to her and how it directly connects to her freedom and self-realization.

Step 3: Action Plan and Shift in Thinking

To deepen her self-compassion, Sara created the following action plan:

- **Communication with her aunt and uncle**: Openly discuss her pressure and her need for privacy, seeking their understanding and cooperation.
- **Create her own time**: As a daily routine, she ensures at least two hours of personal time at home for reading, studying, or video chatting with friends. She also consciously tries to have her own time outside the home (shopping, movies, chatting with friends).
- **Emotion Monitoring**: Continuously record her daily emotions to manage them better.

Results and Changes

Through this process, Sara became more sensitive to her emotions and learned how to respond to them. Dialogue with her aunt and uncle deepened their understanding of her needs, and the family began to respect her privacy. By accepting her emotions and firmly securing her own time, Sara regained her peace of mind. Her new family life became smoother, with no more frustrations, allowing her to remain calm.

Self-compassion is a powerful antidote to the inner critic. We can transform our inner dialogue by practicing self-kindness, recognizing our shared humanity, and being mindful of our experiences. This shift silences the inner critic and fosters emotional well-being and resilience. As you continue to practice self-compassion, you will find that your relationship with yourself becomes more supportive and nurturing, paving the way for greater self-love and acceptance.

Mini Actions You Can Take: 3.5

When you face challenging situations or setbacks, remind yourself, "It's okay; this happens to everyone." Then, write in your diary like you're talking to a close friend. Fill the pages with understanding, praise, and encouragement for yourself. You don't need to share it with anyone. Be generous with your self-praise. Doing this will improve your self-understanding and self-acceptance.

CHAPTER 4

PRACTICING DAILY SELF-LOVE

Waking up to the sound of your alarm, you might feel the day's weight pressing down on you before you even get out of bed. The thoughts start to swirl: the tasks you need to complete, the challenges you anticipate, and the inner critic already whispering doubts. Imagine, though, if your mornings began differently. Instead of rushing into chaos, you start with a gentle, deliberate routine that nurtures your mind and body. How you start your day can set the tone for everything that follows, creating a foundation of self-love and positivity.

4.1 MORNING RITUALS FOR SELF-LOVE: STARTING YOUR DAY POSITIVELY

Morning rituals are more than just habits. They are intentional practices that can shape your mindset for the entire day. When you begin your day with positive routines, you create a sense of control and purpose. This control helps you navigate the challenges that come your way with a calm and focused mind. The psychological benefits of morning rituals are profound. They reduce stress by providing a structured start to your day and boost your mood by incorporating activities that make you feel good about yourself.

One practical morning routine is to practice gratitude as soon as you wake up. Before you even get out of bed, take a moment to think about three things you are grateful for. This simple act can shift your mindset from what you lack to what you have, filling you with a sense of abundance. Setting daily intentions or goals is another powerful practice. Instead of diving into your to-do list, spend a few minutes reflecting on what you want to achieve or how you want to feel that day. These intentions can guide your actions and decisions, helping you stay focused and aligned with your values.

A short mindfulness practice can also set a positive tone for your day. Spend five to ten minutes in quiet reflection, focusing on your breath or repeating a positive affirmation. This practice can help calm your mind, reduce anxiety, and foster a sense of inner peace. For example, you might sit comfortably, close your eyes, and repeat the affirmation, "I am worthy of love and respect." This simple practice can anchor you in a positive mindset, making it easier to face the day confidently.

Incorporating physical activity into your morning routine can boost your self-esteem and energy. Gentle stretching can awaken your body and mind, preparing you for the day ahead. A short walk or jog can invigorate your senses and clear your mind. Even a few minutes of deep breathing exercises can help you feel more centered and energized. Physical activity releases endorphins, which are natural mood boosters. Starting your day with movement can make you feel more capable and resilient.

Consider the story of Sarah, who used to start her mornings in a rush, feeling overwhelmed before she even left the house. She decided to transform her morning routine by incorporating gratitude journaling. She wrote down three things she was grateful for each morning and three goals for the day. This practice helped her focus on the positive aspects of her life and set clear intentions. Over time, Sarah felt calmer and in control, even on busy days. Her morning ritual became a source of strength and positivity.

Another example is Mia, who struggled with chaotic mornings that left her feeling stressed and frazzled. She created a peaceful morning ritual that included gentle stretching and a deep, slow breathing technique. Mia found that these practices helped her start the day with a sense of calm and clarity. She felt more grounded and better equipped to handle the day's challenges. Her morning ritual became a cherished part of her self-care routine, enhancing her overall well-being.

Morning rituals can transform the way you experience your day. By starting with practices that promote self-love and positivity, you create a strong foundation for facing whatever comes your way. Whether you practice gratitude, set intentions, or engage in physical activity, these routines can help you feel more in control, focused, and resilient.

Mini Actions You Can Take: 4.1

Spend five minutes each morning stretching and verbally expressing three things you are grateful for, along with things you want to be mindful of throughout the day, such as spending the day with a smile or not criticizing others. These five minutes can purify your mind and allow you to spend the day feeling refreshed.

4.2 THE POWER OF GRATITUDE: DAILY PRACTICES FOR A POSITIVE MINDSET

Practicing gratitude can profoundly shift your mindset and enhance emotional well-being. When you focus on what you're grateful for, you invite positive energy into your life. Gratitude helps you see the good, even in challenging times. It can lift your spirits, foster a sense of contentment, and reduce negative emotions. Mentally, gratitude acts as a buffer against stress and anxiety. It shifts your focus from what you lack to what you have, promoting a positive outlook on life. This shift can improve your mental health, making you more resilient to daily stressors.

A gratitude journal is a simple yet effective way to incorporate gratitude into daily life. Each day, take a few minutes to write down three things you're grateful for. It doesn't have to be grand; even small things like a sunny day or a kind word from a friend can make a difference. This practice can help you start or end your day on a positive note, reinforcing a mindset of abundance.

Expressing gratitude through letters or notes is another powerful exercise. Write a heartfelt letter to someone who has positively impacted your life. This act strengthens your relationship and reinforces your sense of gratitude. Practicing gratitude during meals can also be transformative.

Before you eat, please take a moment to appreciate the food on your plate and the effort that went into preparing it. This simple practice can deepen your appreciation for life's daily blessings.

The science behind gratitude supports its benefits. Research has shown that gratitude can increase happiness and improve mental health. A study published in the Journal of Happiness Studies found that people who kept a gratitude journal experienced higher levels of happiness and lower levels of depression. Another study from the National Institutes of Health revealed that practicing gratitude can reduce stress by lowering cortisol levels, the hormone associated with stress. These findings highlight the powerful impact gratitude can have on your emotional well-being.

Consider the story of Emily, who struggled with depression for years. She felt trapped in a cycle of negative thoughts and hopelessness. Emily decided to start a gratitude journal as a last resort. She wrote down three things she was grateful for each night, no matter how small. Over time, Emily noticed a shift in her mindset. She began to see the positive aspects of her life that she had previously overlooked. This simple practice helped her break free from the grip of depression and find a renewed sense of hope and happiness.

Another inspiring example is Sarah, who used gratitude to strengthen her relationships. Sarah had always felt distant from her family and friends, often focusing on their flaws rather than their positive quali-ties. She wrote gratitude letters to her loved ones, expressing appreci-ation for their support and kindness. This gratitude brought her closer to her family and friends, deepening her connections and fostering a sense of belonging. Through appreciation, Sarah trans-formed her relationships and created a more supportive and loving environment.

Gratitude has the power to change your perspective and improve your overall well-being. By incorporating gratitude exercises into your daily life, you can cultivate a positive mindset and enhance your emotional health. These simple acts can make a profound difference, whether keeping a gratitude journal, writing letters, or practicing gratitude during meals. The science behind gratitude underscores its benefits, showing that it can increase happiness, reduce stress, and improve mental health. Real-life stories of individuals like Emily and Sarah illustrate the transformative power of gratitude, offering hope and inspiration.

Mini Actions You Can Take: 4.2

Before each meal, close your eyes and think of things you are grateful for.

Throughout the day, try to say "thank you" to as many people as possible, even for the small stuff.

4.3 MINDFULNESS: TECHNIQUES FOR INNER PEACE

Mindfulness is a practice that can profoundly impact your emotional and mental well-being. Mindfulness is the art of being present in the moment, fully engaged with what you're doing, and aware of your thoughts and feelings without judgment. It's about paying attention with intention. The principles of mindfulness are simple yet transformative: focus on the present, observe your thoughts and feelings, and accept them without trying to change them.

Incorporating mindfulness into your daily life can start with simple exercises. Mindful breathing is one of the most accessible practices. Find a quiet spot, sit comfortably, and focus on your breath. Notice the sensation of the air entering and leaving your nostrils. If your mind wanders, gently bring it back to your breath. This practice can be done for a few minutes daily, significantly reducing stress and improving focus.

Mindful eating is another way to bring mindfulness into your daily routine. When you eat, take time to savor each bite. Notice the flavors, textures, and aromas of your food. Chew slowly and appreciate the nourishment it provides. This practice enhances your eating experience and helps you develop a healthier relationship with food. It encourages you to listen to your body's hunger and fullness signals, promoting mindful and intuitive eating.

One thing that significantly disturbs inner peace is anger. Many people feel anger when they are criticized. The anger may linger in the heart for days, weeks, or, in severe cases, even years, making them uncomfortable.

So, how should you deal with anger caused by criticism? When people are criticized, most of them get angry. Why do you think that is?

One reason is criticism aimed solely at attacking the other person without considering their feelings or situation. In such cases, the criticizer should rightfully be asked to apologize.

Another reason is when people realize that at least 10% of the content of the criticism is true. They get angry because it exposes a flaw they want to hide. People want to believe that others see only their strengths and are unaware of their flaws. For instance, if you tell someone conscious about being too thin, "You are overweight. Why don't you go on a diet?" this comment would not hurt the person. They would likely wonder what else about them you dislike, aware that they are not overweight. However, what if the person is overweight and considering losing weight? They would feel offended and angry because they know the truth in the criticism.

This is an extreme example, but when you feel angry due to criticism, try to calm down and consider, "The fact that I am upset means that there's probably 10% truth in what this person is saying." Review the content of the criticism; you are likely to find something that resonates. Then, view this adverse event of criticism as an opportunity, and instead of blaming the other person, transform it into something positive that can serve as fertilizer for your growth.

Another method is to ask yourself, "Will I still be upset about this criticism ten years from now?" If the answer is "No," then like Santa Claus unloading a sack full of grievances, drop it from your shoulders right now and live lightly and freely. If you find it's not so easy to forget, this is when mindfulness, the technique of immersing yourself in the present task, proves helpful. Every time feelings of anger towards criticism surface, shake them off and train yourself to focus on the task. This practice helps prevent external criticisms from disturbing your peace of mind and protects your inner tranquility. As you repeat this technique, you will notice that your anger diminishes over time.

If guilt prevents you from finding inner peace, imagine you've done something regrettable. You might have hurt someone with harsh words or caused harm due to negligence. Overwhelmed with guilt, you might struggle to forgive yourself, possibly for many years.

Here's a method to help you move beyond this deep-seated guilt.

Separate the "bad action" from "yourself." You are not a bad person for making a mistake; you are simply human, capable of errors like anyone else.

Visualize placing the "bad action" in a box and setting it before you. Then, sincerely ask for forgiveness from a higher power, acknowledging your deep regret and apologizing for your actions. Repeat this process until you feel at peace. Once you feel your apology has been accepted, request a transformation:

"Please transform what is in this box from a painful truth into a catalyst for becoming a more compassionate person who can help others suffering similarly."

Affirm that you will use the lessons contained within this box. When you feel the contents have transformed, take the box to a garden named "you" and spread it like fertilizer.

Then declare: "I am reborn. I will live a life that uplifts and encourages others."

This process aims to turn your suffering into something beautiful—an inner beauty not meant to impress others outwardly but to heal and enlighten those around you. This privilege isn't for the chosen few; it's a responsibility you accept to transform your past mistakes into lessons that help others. Embrace this mission passionately, as only your warmth can bring warmth to others, helping them rediscover smiles and warmth in their hearts.

Mini Actions You Can Take: 4.3

You can feel as heated as a boiling kettle when anger bubbles up inside you. It's hard to make good decisions in such a state, so first, you must cool down. Imagine yourself diving into a swimming pool when you're overwhelmed by anger. Relax in the water and gaze up at the blue sky. Lay the issue that angered you out on a table and look at it from different angles. For instance, consider whether the other person meant to harm you or if there were factors you weren't aware of. Consider what advice you would give a friend in the same situation. Everyone has different values and approaches; not everything will align with yours. Approach the situation calmly. And when you get out of the swimming pool, remind yourself: "I am not controlled by what happens to me. I control how I respond."

4.4 VISUALIZATION TECHNIQUES FOR SELF-CONFIDENCE

Visualization is a powerful mental tool that creates vivid images of desired outcomes in your mind. It's about imagining yourself achieving your goals and experiencing the emotions of that success. This technique can be incredibly effective in building self-confidence. When you visualize yourself succeeding, your brain starts to believe it's possible, which boosts your motivation and self-belief. You create mental images of what you want to achieve, whether it's delivering a presentation, mastering a new skill, or gracefully navigating a challenging situation. By seeing these images in your mind, you lay the groundwork for making them a reality.

The psychological and emotional benefits of visualization are well-documented. Visualization enhances motivation by clearly showing your goals and the steps needed. This clarity helps you stay focused and committed, even when faced with obstacles. Visualization also reduces anxiety by familiarizing your mind with the desired outcome, making it feel more attainable. When you repeatedly visualize success, you build a sense of self-belief that counteracts self-doubt. This practice helps you approach challenges with confidence, knowing that you have already seen yourself succeed in your mind.

An experiment on the effects of visualization was conducted at a high school. The school's basketball team was divided into three groups, and the experiment assessed which team could score the most shots after two weeks. Group A was instructed not to practice at all for two weeks. Group B was told not to practice but to visualize themselves making daily shots. Group C practiced shooting at a designated time every day. The results showed that Group B made the most shots, followed by Group C and Group A. This is a fascinating study. Similar experiments have been conducted, and the results are always the same. This suggests that when repeatedly visualizing something, the brain inputs it and judges whether it should be so.

I have a friend whose son excels in judo. He has been in a black belt for a long time and has participated in many tournaments. He was enamored with a particularly high-level technique and watched videos of it repeatedly. However, it was a complicated technique, and he had never practiced it. He used this complex technique during a tournament he had never practiced before and won the competition. Everyone was surprised, especially him.

Finally, let me share another real-life example. A university student had a vision board with pictures of a car and a house he wanted to own one day, which he looked at daily. He set goals to own this car and live in a beautiful home as he studied. A few years after graduating, he acquired the car of his dreams. Over time, he started a family and forgot about the vision board. When he moved from a rented house to his own, he found the vision board from his university days in a cardboard box and was amazed. The house he had bought was pictured on the board beside the house number next to the door.

This might surprise us, but from a neuroscience perspective, it's natural. When we imprint a vision onto our brain, it does not distinguish between fantasy and reality. Thus, it becomes a reality.

To get started with visualization:

1. Try a confidence visualization exercise.
2. Find a quiet place where you won't be disturbed.
3. Close your eyes and take a few deep breaths to calm your mind.
4. Imagine yourself in a situation where you want to feel confident.

It could be giving a speech, interviewing, or handling a difficult conversation. Picture every detail vividly: what you're wearing, the expressions on people's faces, and the sound of your voice. See yourself handling the situation with ease and confidence. Feel the emotions associated with this success—pride, happiness, and satisfaction. Spend a few minutes each day practicing this visualization; over time, you'll notice a boost in your self-confidence.

Another effective exercise is future self-visualization. This involves imagining a future version of yourself who has achieved your goals and embodies your desired qualities. Again, find a quiet place to sit comfortably. Close your eyes and visualize your future self in as much detail as possible. See yourself living the life you dream of, having accomplished your goals. Notice how you carry yourself, how you interact with others, and how you feel. Picture the confident, successful version of yourself and note the steps your future self took to get there. This exercise boosts your confidence and provides a roadmap for your actions.

Integrating visualization into your daily routine is both simple and effective. You can set aside a few minutes each day for visualization, making it a part of your morning or evening routine. The key is consistency, so make it a regular habit. You can also use visualization before important events or tasks. For instance, if you have a significant meeting or presentation, take a few moments to visualize yourself performing confidently and successfully. This mental rehearsal can help reduce anxiety and enhance your performance, making visualization a versatile tool in your self-improvement arsenal.

Consider the story of Anna, a professional who struggled with self-doubt before essential work meetings. She decided to try visualization to boost her confidence. Each morning, she spent five minutes visualizing herself leading meetings with poise and confidence. She pictured herself speaking clearly, making eye contact, and receiving positive feedback from her colleagues. Over time, Anna noticed a significant improvement in her confidence levels. She felt more at ease during meetings and could effectively present her ideas.

Visualization became a crucial part of her self-confidence toolkit, helping her thrive professionally. Anna's story is a testament to the transformative power of visualization, inspiring us to incorporate this practice into our self-improvement journey.

Visualization techniques offer a practical and powerful way to build self-confidence. Imagine successful outcomes and create mental images of your goals to enhance your motivation and focus. Guided visualization exercises, such as confidence and future self-visualization, provide a structured approach to this practice. Incorporating visualization into your daily routine can help you reduce anxiety, boost self-belief, and approach challenges with greater confidence. Whether preparing for a specific event or looking to improve your overall self-esteem, visualization can be a valuable tool in your self-love journey.

Mini Actions You Can Take: 4.4

In the morning, in front of the mirror, and when you lie down in bed at night, vividly imagine the situation you desire in detail. Also, vividly imagine yourself feeling cheerful and lively in that moment.

Please set up a vision board in your bedroom and clearly post the things and situations you desire on it. Be sure to look at it every morning when you get ready and every night before you go to bed.

4.5 SELF-DISCOVERY: JOURNALING / JOHARI WINDOW

Journaling

Journaling is an effective tool for self-discovery and emotional healing. It enables individuals to deeply explore their thoughts and emotions, offering unique opportunities for personal insight and growth. Here are some journaling techniques and prompts that could be helpful:

- **Stream-of-consciousness writing**: This technique involves writing continuously for 5 to 10 minutes without stopping to edit or organize thoughts. It can reveal underlying emotions or ideas that are often overlooked in daily life.
- **Reflective journaling with prompts**: Prompts can direct your attention to specific areas of life you wish to explore or improve. Questions like "What lessons did I learn today?" or "What emotions did I feel today, and why?" help deepen your understanding of experiences, promoting growth and self-awareness.
- **Gratitude journaling**: Regularly documenting things you are grateful for can shift your focus from what you lack to what you have, enhancing your overall well-being. Prompts such as "What made me smile today?" or "Who am I grateful for, and why?" effectively foster a gratitude mindset.

- **Goal-oriented journaling**: This method involves writing about your goals, the steps needed to achieve them, and any potential obstacles. It helps keep you accountable and clarifies your path forward. Prompts like "What are my goals for next month?" or "What can I do today to move closer to my goals?" can be very helpful.
- **Emotional release journaling**: Sometimes, venting or processing intense emotions is necessary. Journaling can be particularly therapeutic in such situations. Prompts like "What is weighing on my mind right now?" or "What fears did I face today, and how did I handle them?" can be especially beneficial.

Johari Window

The Johari Window is a psychological model designed to enhance self-awareness, developed in 1961 by American psychologists Joseph Luft and Harry Ingham. It facilitates deeper personal self-awareness through 'self-disclosure' and 'feedback.' The Johari Window includes four areas:

- **Open Area**: Traits or information that both the individual and others know.
- **Blind Spot**: Traits or information that the individual is unaware of, but others recognize.
- **Hidden Area**: Traits or information that the individual is aware of but has not disclosed to others.
- **Unknown Area**: Traits or information that neither the individual nor others know.

The Johari Window is primarily used to deepen self-awareness through self-disclosure and feedback. Here are the specific steps involved:

Promoting Self-Disclosure:

By intentionally sharing information or emotions about yourself that others may not know, you can reduce your "hidden area" and expand your "open area."

- Sharing your hobbies, past experiences, and challenges with team members or friends can be enlightening.
- Revealing your shortcomings to a close friend and sharing what you do to overcome them.

Actively Seeking Feedback:

Receiving others' feedback on your behavior or traits can help uncover your "blind spots" and increase your "open area."

- After a presentation, asking for feedback from colleagues or supervisors can help you identify strengths and areas needing improvement.
- Asking a close friend about your strengths and weaknesses.

Exploring the Unknown Area:

Participating in new experiences, training sessions, or psychological tests can reveal traits or abilities ("unknown area") that neither you nor others are aware of, which can open new aspects of self-awareness and contribute to personal growth.

- Engaging in new hobbies or skills, like photography, dancing, or programming, can help you discover new interests or talents.
- Psychological tests like the MBTI or DISC assessments can provide insights into unrecognized characteristics or tendencies.
- Seizing opportunities to lead, especially if they are outside

your usual role, can expose your leadership qualities and how you handle challenging situations.

Promoting Dialogue and Empathy:

Deepening mutual understanding through conversations with others can expand the "open area" for both parties. This involves actively listening and showing empathy.

- Practice active listening. Focus on words and nonverbal cues, such as facial expressions and gestures, which can deepen understanding and improve responses.
- Employ empathy statements: Expressing understanding and empathy, such as saying, "That must have been tough," or "How did that feel?" can help build trust.

Employing the Johari Window in these ways can enhance self-awareness and provide valuable insights that aid in self-improvement. It can also strengthen relationships and improve communication with others.

Mini Actions You Can Take: 4.5

Try keeping a journal with prompts and enjoy the process of journaling. By focusing more on yourself, you'll notice your mood improving and your thoughts becoming more positive.

4.6 CELEBRATING SMALL WINS: RECOGNIZING YOUR ACHIEVEMENTS

Recognizing your achievements, no matter how small, is crucial for building self-esteem and self-worth. When you acknowledge your progress, you reinforce positive behavior and habits, which helps to solidify them. This acknowledgment creates a psychological impact that boosts your confidence and motivates you to keep going.

Celebrating small wins is like giving yourself a pat on the back; it reassures you that you are on the right path and that your efforts are paying off. This practice can shift your focus from what you haven't achieved to what you have, fostering a sense of accomplishment and pride.

One practical way to celebrate your achievements is by keeping a "success jar." Each time you accomplish something, write it down on a small piece of paper and place it in the jar. Over time, this jar becomes a tangible representation of your progress. On days when you feel down or doubtful, you can revisit these notes to remind yourself of how far you've come. Sharing your accomplishments with a supportive friend or group can also be incredibly validating. When you share your wins, you invite others to celebrate with you, which can amplify the positive feelings and provide additional encouragement.

Creating a visual board of milestones is another effective method. This board can include photos, quotes, and notes that represent your achievements. Place it somewhere you'll see it daily to serve as a constant reminder of your capabilities and progress. These visual cues can be powerful motivators, keeping your goals in sight and your achievements top of mind.

The benefits of celebrating small wins extend beyond immediate gratification. This practice builds momentum for larger goals, making the journey toward them more manageable and less daunting. Each small win acts as a steppingstone, giving you the confidence to tackle bigger challenges. By celebrating these incremental successes, you enhance your self-efficacy—the belief in your ability to succeed. This growing sense of self-belief can transform your mindset from one of doubt and uncertainty to one of confidence and determination.

Consider the story of Amanda, who struggled with self-doubt and low self-esteem. She decided to start keeping a success jar. Whenever she completed a task, no matter how small, she wrote it down and added it to the jar. Over weeks and months, Amanda's jar filled up with notes of her achievements. On tough days, she would read through them and remind herself of her progress. This practice helped Amanda shift her focus from her perceived failures to her real successes, gradually transforming her self-perception.

Another inspiring example is Lisa, who faced daily challenges at work and often felt overwhelmed. She decided to create a visual board of her milestones. Each time she achieved a goal or received positive feedback; she added it to her board. This visual reminder helped Lisa see the bigger picture and recognize her growth. Celebrating these daily achievements boosted her motivation and confidence, allowing her to tackle more significant projects with a renewed sense of self-belief.

Celebrating small wins is a simple yet powerful practice that can significantly impact your self-esteem and motivation. Recognizing and honoring your achievements creates a positive feedback loop that reinforces your progress and encourages further growth. Whether through a success jar, sharing with friends, or making a visual board, these practices can help you build momentum, enhance self-efficacy, and transform your self-perception. Taking the time to celebrate your wins, no matter how small, is an act of self-love that acknowledges your worth and capabilities.

This chapter explored ways to practice daily self-love, from morning rituals to celebrating small wins. Each practice is a building block for enhancing self-worth and fostering a positive mindset.

As we move forward, we'll discuss the importance of setting and maintaining healthy boundaries, a crucial aspect of self-love that ensures one's well-being is protected and respected.

Mini Actions You Can Take: 4.6

Create a visual milestone board and decide how you will celebrate achieving your goals. Consider exciting things like eating your favorite cake at a cafe with friends, enjoying wine at a seaside restaurant, or attending a concert. Thinking about these enjoyable activities will also contribute to your happiness.

CHAPTER 5

SETTING AND MAINTAINING HEALTHY BOUNDARIES

Boundaries are personal limits that protect your physical, emotional, and mental space. Think of them as the invisible lines that define where you end, and others begin. They act as safeguards, ensuring you maintain control over your life. Boundaries come in various forms: physical, emotional, mental, and time related. Physical boundaries pertain to your personal space and physical touch. Emotional boundaries involve your feelings and how much emotional energy you give to others. Mental boundaries refer to your thoughts, beliefs, and opinions. Time-related boundaries determine how you allocate your time and energy.

5.1 THE IMPORTANCE OF BOUNDARIES: PROTECTING YOUR WELL-BEING

Setting boundaries is not just about keeping others out but protecting your well-being. When you establish clear boundaries, you create a sense of self-respect and self-care. Boundaries help protect your mental health by reducing stress and preventing burnout. They allow you to say no to things that drain you and yes to things that nourish you. This self-assertion enhances your self-esteem because you begin to see yourself as worthy of care and respect. Moreover, boundaries foster healthier and more respectful relationships. Communicating with your limits teaches others how to treat you, leading to more balanced and fulfilling interactions.

Failing to set or maintain boundaries can have serious consequences. Without boundaries, you are more likely to experience burnout and emotional exhaustion. When you constantly put others' needs before your own, you deplete your energy reserves, leaving little for self-care. This lack of boundaries also increases the risk of being taken advantage of or manipulated. People may see you as an easy target for their demands and expectations, further eroding your self-worth. The resulting feelings of resentment and frustration can strain your relationships and negatively impact your overall well-being.

Imagine a woman named Lisa who always says yes when she means no. She agrees to extra work, social events she dreads, and favors that drain her energy. Over time, Lisa feels exhausted, resentful, and disconnected from her needs. She wonders why she feels overwhelmed and that her relationships are so one-sided. You're not alone if you've ever been in Lisa's shoes. Many women struggle with setting boundaries, but learning to establish and maintain them is crucial for your well-being.

This is the story of Sarah, a hardworking IT consultant who often worked late at night as project deadlines approached. Recognizing the negative impact this was having on her health and family life, Sarah resolved to set work-life balance boundaries. She explained to her boss that working within regular hours was the most efficient way to complete tasks. They agreed that Sarah could leave work on time every day. This boundary setting allowed Sarah to spend her evenings refreshing herself and spending time with her family, which reclaimed her personal time and improved her work efficiency.

Another example is the story of Jenny, who was exhausted by a relationship with a friend who constantly made critical comments. Jenny felt emotionally and physically drained after each interaction. Therefore, she decided to set emotional boundaries by limiting her contact with this friend. Jenny communicated her desire for a respectful relationship with her friend and informed her that she would distance herself if the friend did not change. As the friend continued her toxic behavior, Jenny made the tough decision to reduce their interactions. This boundary protected Jenny's emotional health, allowing her to focus on cultivating relationships that were uplifting.

Setting boundaries is an act of self-love and empowerment. It requires recognizing your worth and prioritizing your health. Start by identifying areas in your life where you feel overburdened or

ignored. Reflect on what you need to feel safe and valued. Confidently communicate your boundaries and remember that it is okay to say no. Setting boundaries is not about being selfish; it is about ensuring you have the energy and emotional resources needed to be your best self. Protecting your well-being lays the foundation for a healthier, more fulfilling life.

Mini Actions You Can Take: 5.1

- First, identify the areas where you want to establish boundaries.
- Then, bravely propose these to the other person. Begin by sharing the positive aspects, like how much you enjoy and appreciate your time together.
- After that, explain the boundaries you'd like to set to protect your privacy. Remember that this isn't about placing blame but enhancing your relationship to keep it healthy.
- Express gratitude and show respect in your approach; your words will likely be received more quickly than expected.

5.2 IDENTIFYING BOUNDARY VIOLATIONS: RECOGNIZING RED FLAGS

Boundary violations occur when someone disregards your limits, intentionally or unintentionally. These actions or behaviors overstep your boundaries, impacting your well-being. When someone intrudes on your personal space, disregards your preferences, or manipulates you, it can leave you feeling vulnerable and disrespected. The emotional toll of boundary violations is significant, often resulting in feelings of anxiety, frustration, and a diminished sense of self-worth. Recognizing these violations is the first step toward reclaiming your personal space and emotional health.

Common red flags that indicate boundary violations include persistent personal space or privacy intrusion. For example, someone might go through your belongings without permission, listen to your private conversations, or invade your physical space. Disregarding personal preferences or needs is another red flag. This could manifest as someone pressuring you to engage in uncomfortable activities or dismissing your feelings and desires. Manipulative or controlling behavior is also a clear sign of boundary violations. This might involve someone trying to dictate your actions, making you feel guilty for asserting your needs, or using emotional manipulation to get their way.

Engaging in self-reflection exercises is essential to help you recognize your boundaries. Start by identifying situations where you feel uncomfortable, stressed, or disrespected. Reflect on what specifically made you feel that way. For example, feeling uneasy when someone stands too close to you could indicate a need for stronger physical boundaries. Keeping a journal to track boundary violations can also be helpful. Write down instances where you felt your boundaries were crossed, noting how you reacted and the outcome. This practice can reveal patterns and help you understand your limits more clearly.

Consider the scenario of a friend who constantly demands your time and attention. This friend calls you multiple times a day, expects you to drop everything to meet their needs, and becomes upset when you don't comply. Over time, you feel drained and resentful, realizing that this behavior violates your emotional boundaries.

Another example could involve a family member disregarding your personal space and privacy. They enter your room without knocking, go through your items, and dismiss your requests for privacy. This persistent intrusion leaves you feeling disrespected and frustrated.

Recognizing these boundary violations in both scenarios is crucial for protecting your well-being. It allows you to identify the behaviors that make you uncomfortable and take steps to address them. Understanding your limits and when they are being crossed will enable you to assert your boundaries more effectively, ensuring that your emotional and physical space is respected.

Mini Actions You Can Take: 5.2

When someone repeatedly invades your personal space or privacy, it's essential to take the time to sit down and discuss it with them. Having a third party present during this conversation can help keep emotions in check. For instance, if your younger brother keeps messing up your room without permission, having someone older, like your father or an older brother, act as a mediator would be helpful.

5.3 COMMUNICATING BOUNDARIES EFFECTIVELY: SCRIPTS AND STRATEGIES

Clear communication is the backbone of effective boundary-setting. When you express your boundaries clearly and assertively, you set expectations and prevent misunderstandings. This clarity fosters mutual respect in relationships, helping others understand your needs and limits. Without it, even well-intentioned people might inadvertently overstep, leading to frustration and resentment. Think of it as drawing a line in the sand; the more precise the line, the less likely it is to be crossed.

One effective strategy for communicating boundaries is using "I" statements. These statements allow you to express your needs and feelings without sounding accusatory. For example, instead of saying, "You never give me any space," you might say, "I need some alone time to recharge; I'll be available after 6 PM." This approach focuses on your needs rather than blaming the other person, making it easier for them to understand and respect your boundaries.

Being direct and specific about what is acceptable and what is not is also crucial. Vague statements can lead to misinterpretations and unintentional boundary violations. Clearly state what behavior you find unacceptable and what changes you need. For instance, if someone often shares your personal information without consent, you could say, "Please do not discuss my personal life with others without my consent."

Consistency is key in boundary-setting. Once you communicate your boundaries, you must follow through with consequences if they are violated. This consistency reinforces your boundaries and shows others you protect your well-being seriously. For example, if you've asked a friend not to call you during work hours and they continue to do so, remind them of your boundary and let them know that you will not answer calls during that time. Repeated communication of your boundaries is necessary, especially in the beginning. People might forget or test your boundaries, so gentle reminders help reinforce them. For example, if someone tries to engage in behavior you've already addressed, calmly restate your boundary: "I mentioned that I'm not comfortable with this behavior, and I need it to stop."

Creating scripts for common boundary-setting scenarios can be incredibly helpful. These scripts provide a framework you can adapt to fit your situation. Here are a few examples:

- "I need some time to recharge; I'll be available after 6 PM." This script is useful when setting a boundary around personal time.
- "Please do not discuss my personal life with others without my consent." Use this when someone shares your private information without permission.
- "I am uncomfortable with [specific behavior] and need it to stop." This is a versatile script for addressing any uncomfortable behavior.

These scripts can be customized to fit your unique circumstances. Practice them until they feel natural, and use them as a starting point for your conversations. The more you practice, the more confident you'll be in asserting your boundaries.

It's important to remember that setting boundaries is not a one-time event but an ongoing process. You might face resistance or pushback, but staying consistent is crucial. When you reinforce your boundaries, you strengthen your self-respect and teach others how to treat you. Consistency also helps build self-esteem, as you see yourself standing up for your needs and values. This process can be empowering, transforming how you interact with the world and improving your relationships.

In summary, clear communication is vital for effective boundary-setting. Using "I" statements, being direct and specific, and following through with consequences are essential strategies. Practicing scripts for common scenarios can boost your confidence and help you articulate your needs. Remember, consistency in enforcing boundaries is key to maintaining them and protecting your well-being.

Mini Actions You Can Take: 5.3

Create a script tailored to your situation, similar to the examples below. Prepare it so you can immediately communicate your boundaries the next time they are crossed.

"I need time to recharge. I'll be available after 6 PM." "Please do not talk about my personal life to others without my consent." "I feel uncomfortable with [specific action] and would like you to stop."

5.4 HANDLING PUSHBACK: STANDING FIRM IN YOUR BOUNDARIES

When you start setting boundaries, you might encounter pushbacks. People may resist or challenge your boundaries for several reasons. Often, they are uncomfortable with change and feel a loss of control when you assert your needs. They might have been accustomed to you saying yes to everything and now struggle with the new dynamics. Misunderstanding the importance of boundaries can also lead to resistance. Some people may not realize how crucial boundaries are for maintaining healthy relationships and personal well-being. They might view your new limits as a rejection or an unnecessary barrier rather than a step towards mutual respect.

To handle pushback effectively, it's essential to remain calm and assertive. This can be challenging, especially if you're dealing with someone who is used to crossing your boundaries. Keep your composure and stand firm in your decisions. Remind yourself that setting boundaries is an act of self-respect. When faced with resistance, reiterate the importance of the boundary. For example, you might say, "I understand this is different from what we're used to, but I need this time to recharge." You reinforce the boundary without escalating the situation by calmly restating your needs.

Let's consider Rachel's situation. Rachel lives with her parents and brother, who run their own business. Due to their lengthy business hours, they are always occupied, leaving Rachel, a university student, to handle most of the household chores. She has repeatedly asked her family to help with the chores, but has always been told they're too busy. One evening, after dinner, Rachel called a family meeting to discuss her need for study time. She asked for two afternoons off each week and proposed that her father, mother, and brother each take on some of the chores. Understanding that her request was reasonable, her family agreed to help out.

As a result, Rachel managed to find time for both studying at home and socializing with friends, which helped her maintain a healthy mental state.

Another example is Sarah, who had a friend who constantly relied on her for emotional support, often at inconvenient times. When Sarah started setting boundaries, her friend resisted, accusing her of being selfish. Sarah calmly reiterated that while she valued their friendship, she needed to prioritize her mental health. She suggested scheduling regular catch-ups instead of last-minute, emotionally draining calls. Over time, her friend adjusted to the new dynamic, and their relationship became more balanced and respectful.

During pushback, self-care becomes even more critical. Dealing with resistance can be emotionally taxing, so it's essential to seek support from trusted friends or a therapist. Talking to someone who understands and validates your feelings can provide the emotional strength to stand firm. Stress-relief techniques like mindfulness or physical exercise can also help you stay grounded. Practicing self-compassion is vital; remember that it's okay to prioritize your needs and that maintaining boundaries is a form of self-love.

In these situations, maintaining boundaries is not just about saying no; it's about affirming your right to a healthy and balanced life. Reiterate your boundaries with calm confidence, and don't be afraid to seek support. By practicing self-care and self-compassion, you can navigate pushback with resilience and maintain the boundaries that protect your well-being.

Mini Actions You Can Take: 5.4

When you encounter pushback, the first thing you should do is not react to it. Maintain your composure and present a firm intention with the statement, "I will not change my proposal to protect my boundaries." Show your determination not by raising your voice but by keeping calm, thereby conveying the strength of your will to the other party.

5.5 BOUNDARY SETTING IN RELATIONSHIPS: FRIENDS, FAMILY, AND PARTNERS

Setting boundaries in relationships can be challenging, as each type of relationship has its dynamics and expectations. With friends, the challenge often lies in balancing closeness with personal space. Friends may expect constant availability, but communicating your needs and expectations is crucial.

Example in friendship:

Amanda was overwhelmed by too many messages from her friend Ashley via social media, which infringed on her private time. Amanda decided to inform Ashley that she practices digital detox over the weekends, so her responses to messages would be delayed. By setting this boundary, Amanda could secure her weekends for herself and maintain a healthy relationship with Ashley.

Hannah's friend, Grace, often drops by unannounced. While Hannah enjoys her visits, they frequently interrupt her study time or happen just as she's about to go out. So, Hannah asked Grace to give her a heads-up before coming over. This respects her time and establishes a precedent for mutual respect.

Example in family relationships:

A woman was troubled by her parents' frequent intervention in household chores, compromising her privacy. She discussed this with her family and established a rule that she would manage her room. They also created a schedule for sharing household duties, clarifying everyone's responsibilities. By defining these boundaries, her privacy was protected, and the whole family began to cooperate more in managing the household chores.

In some families, despite a child's desire for independence, parents might overly interfere with everything from choosing a university to managing daily schedules. The child can set boundaries by telling the parents they want to make their own choices. This may help the parents understand the importance of fostering the child's ability to make decisions independently, leading them to offer support without excessive intervention.

Example between couples:

Respecting Privacy: Even within a marriage, respecting each other's privacy is necessary. For instance, it's essential to maintain personal space by not checking each other's cell phones or emails without permission. This helps strengthen the trust between partners and preserves their independence.

Time Management: When one partner needs time for hobbies or personal development, it is crucial to respect this need. For example, by allocating time on weekends for each person to engage in activities they enjoy, both partners can lead more fulfilling lives. This respect for personal time enriches the relationship and supports individual growth.

Setting boundaries for emotional support in marital relationships is crucial for maintaining mental health and strengthening the relationship. Here are the details:

The Importance of Boundaries in Emotional Support: Emotional support is a fundamental aspect of marital relationships, but an imbalance can strain the relationship. If one partner consistently acts as an emotional dumping ground for the other, it can lead to exhaustion and stress, which may cause tension and discord.

How to Seek Appropriate Support: When facing emotional issues or significant decisions, how you ask for support from your partner is essential. Rather than dumping all emotional burdens on them, it's vital to communicate clearly when specific help is needed. For instance, saying, "I just need you to listen right now; I'm not looking for solutions," can prevent overburdening your partner.

Importance of Self-Care: Managing your own emotional needs is also crucial. Practicing self-care and seeking counseling or professional support can help maintain your emotional health without overloading your partner.

Balancing Shared and Personal Time: In emotional support, it is important to balance the time shared together and personal time. Respecting each other's emotions while also taking time alone for self-reflection and relaxation can build a healthier relationship.

By paying attention to these points and setting boundaries around emotional support, couples can appropriately support each other's emotions, safeguard their mental health, and sustain their relationship.

Mini Actions You Can Take: 5.5

- **Setting Boundaries in Digital Communication:** Specify response times and hours for communication via social media and messaging apps and communicate these boundaries to friends. For example, establish rules such as not responding after 9 PM on weekdays and engaging in digital detox over the weekends.

- **Establishing Respect for Privacy at Home:**
  1. Discuss with your family the importance of respecting the privacy of your room and personal time.
  2. Clarify the division of responsibilities in household chores and daily life.
  3. Share specific schedules and rules to create a culture of mutual respect's space.
- **Supporting Independence in Parent-Child Relationships:** Children should clearly communicate their desire for independence to their parents, using specific examples like choosing a college or managing daily schedules. Parents should respect their children's decisions and discuss the extent and method of support they will provide.
- **Securing Personal Time with Your Partner:** Couples or partners should recognize the importance of having hobbies and personal time and make specific agreements to respect each other's needs (e.g., allocating personal time for hobbies once a week).
- **Balancing Emotional Support:** When providing emotional support to your partner, clearly communicate the type of support needed, distinguishing between times when you need to be heard and when you need to seek advice. Also, listen to each other's emotional needs while ensuring time for self-care.

By taking these actions, you can establish healthy boundaries in various relationships and support each other's happiness and growth.

CHAPTER 6

BUILDING SELF-WORTH FROM WITHIN

I magine standing in front of a mirror and genuinely liking the person staring back at you—not just for your appearance but for who you are at your core. This might seem distant or even impossible, but it's the essence of recognizing your inherent worth. Building self-worth is not about external achievements or validations; it's about understanding and appreciating your true self. This chapter aims to guide you through recognizing your inherent worth and understanding the foundation of self-esteem.

6.1 RECOGNIZING YOUR INHERENT WORTH: UNDERSTANDING SELF-ESTEEM

The Difference Between Self-Esteem and Self-Love

Self-Esteem: Self-esteem refers to a positive evaluation and respect for one's worth and abilities. People with high self-esteem recognize their strengths and weaknesses yet still respect and find value in themselves. Self-esteem is based on self-evaluation that comes from within rather than depending on external evaluations.

Self-Love: Self-love means having love for oneself and prioritizing oneself. There are healthy forms of self-love and pathological self-love (narcissism). Healthy self-love includes:

- Self-respect and self-care.
- Accurately assessing oneself.
- Healthily meeting one's needs.

On the other hand, pathological self-love tends to be excessively self-centered and ignores the needs of others.

Self-esteem is a measure of your self-worth and self-respect. It reflects how you see yourself and value your abilities, qualities, and achievements. High self-esteem means you have a favorable opinion of yourself. It involves appreciating your worth and importance while being accountable and acting responsibly toward others. Nathaniel Brandon, a renowned psychologist, defines self-esteem as having confidence in one's ability to cope with life's challenges and feeling worthy of success and happiness. When you have healthy self-esteem, you believe in your ability to navigate life's obstacles and feel deserving of joy and accomplishment.

Recognizing your inherent worth is crucial for your overall mental and emotional health. Self-esteem influences various aspects of life, including your workplace behavior, relationships, and overall happiness. High self-esteem is associated with positive qualities such as realism, creativity, independence, and cooperativeness. On the other hand, low self-esteem is linked to negative traits like rigidity, fear of the unfamiliar, defensiveness, and hostility. Healthy self-esteem makes you more likely to take appropriate risks, pursue opportunities, and build fulfilling relationships. You become more resilient and better equipped to handle stress and setbacks.

The sources of self-esteem are diverse and develop over time. Childhood experiences and parental influence play a significant role. Children who feel valued and supported are more likely to develop high self-esteem. Parents who set fair limits, respect their child's dignity, and have high behavioral expectations contribute positively to their child's self-worth. Achievements and personal successes also boost self-esteem. Accomplishing goals, receiving recognition, and overcoming challenges reinforce your belief in your abilities. Social interactions and relationships further shape your self-esteem. Positive relationships where you feel loved, respected, and valued enhance your self-worth. Conversely, negative interactions can erode it.

Understanding the difference between healthy and unhealthy self-esteem is essential. Healthy self-esteem is consistent and internal. It means you value yourself regardless of external circumstances. You have a stable sense of self-worth that doesn't fluctuate based on others' opinions or achievements. Unhealthy self-esteem, however, is dependent on external validation. It's unstable and fluctuates with feedback from others. If your self-worth relies on praise or approval, it can lead to anxiety and insecurity. You may constantly seek validation, and any criticism or failure can cause significant distress.

Recognizing where you stand on the self-esteem spectrum can be enlightening. Recognizing where you stand on the self-esteem spectrum can be an enlightening experience. It shows various stages and characteristics, from very low to very high self-esteem. Here are ten specific examples. These examples illustrate different thoughts, feelings, and behaviors associated with varying degrees of self-esteem:

1. **Very Low Self-Esteem:**
   - Believe they will fail no matter what they do and are afraid of trying new things.
2. **Low Self-Esteem:**
   - Constantly fear criticism from others and cannot express their opinions or feelings.
3. **Slightly Low Self-Esteem:**
   - Do not attribute success to their efforts but believe it is due to luck (impostor syndrome).
4. **Moderately Low Average Self-Esteem:**
   - Recognizes their abilities to some extent but often suffers from self-doubt.
5. **Neutral Self-Esteem:**
   - Realistically assess their abilities and limitations but occasionally need more confidence.
6. **Slightly High Self-Esteem:**
   - Generally recognizes their value and is not shaken by criticism from others, but avoids overconfidence.
7. **High Self-Esteem:**
   - Sincerely believe in themselves and their abilities, maintaining a sense of self-efficacy even when faced with difficulties.
8. **Quite High Self-Esteem:**
   - Acknowledges their value and the value of others, building balanced, supportive relationships.

9. **Very High Self-Esteem**:
   - Has very strong self-affirmation and complete confidence in their decisions and actions.
10. **Excessive Self-Esteem (Narcissistic Tendency)**:
    - Overestimates their abilities and values and tends to ignore the opinions and feelings of others.

These spectrum examples demonstrate how individual self-esteem can vary. For those with very low self-esteem, seeking psychological support or counseling can be beneficial. Conversely, those with excessive self-esteem might need to adjust their relationships with others and learn humility.

Reflective journaling prompts are another practical method. Writing about your feelings, experiences, and perceptions can reveal patterns and areas where your self-esteem might be lacking.

Reflective journaling prompts are questions and themes designed to facilitate self-reflection. They serve as tools to help individuals deeply think about and document their feelings, experiences, actions, and thoughts. Through this process, individuals can enhance self-awareness and understand behavior patterns and emotional responses. Prompts typically include specific questions or instructions that guide writing in a diary or journal.

For example, here are some types of reflective journaling prompts:

- "Write in detail about the emotions you felt today. What specific situation caused these emotions?"
  - This prompt helps us understand the circumstances and causes behind specific emotions.
- "What past decision are you still proud of today? What did you learn from that decision?"
  - This increases self-affirmation and reaffirms lessons learned from past successes.

- "If you could turn back time, is there a moment where you would make a different choice? Why?"
  - This prompt involves reflecting on past choices, examining why a different decision might have been made, and how it impacts the present.
- "Visualize your ideal future. What can you do now to work towards that ideal?"
  - Focus on long-term goals and dreams, and consider realistic steps towards achieving them.
- "What have you learned from a recent challenging experience? How did you handle it?"
  - Reflect on insights gained and methods of coping during difficult situations.
- "How do you think you influence others? Provide specific examples of how your actions have impacted those around you."
  - This helps understand one's social impact and explores how one's actions affect others.

Incorporating these prompts into daily journaling can deepen self-understanding and promote personal growth.

Reflective journaling is a process that involves writing down your thoughts and reflections on specific prompts or questions. After writing down your answers to the prompts I provided, here are some steps you might consider:

Review and Reflect: Read over what you've written. See if you notice any patterns or recurring themes in your responses.

- **Example:** Review the journals written during the week and analyze your stressed behaviors. For instance, if you notice that you always feel irritated before meetings, you can explore the reasons and consider how to handle them.

Deeper Analysis: Think about what your answers say about you. For example, how do your core values impact your daily decisions? Are there discrepancies between what you value and how you act?

- **Example:** In your self-assessment, even though you value 'helping others,' you realize that you often don't have time for friends seeking help. Understanding this discrepancy, you consider how to balance it.

Set Goals: Based on your reflections, identify areas for personal growth. Set specific, achievable goals that align with your values and what you've learned about yourself.

- **Example:** To actively engage in self-care, set specific goals, such as setting aside time to read a favorite book each week as a reward or booking a massage or spa visit once a month.

Plan Actions: Develop a plan for how to meet these goals. This could involve changing behaviors, seeking new experiences, or continuing education.

- **Example:** Plan to refresh mentally by starting a new hobby, such as joining a watercolor painting class—research class schedules, including participation costs and transportation plans in your planning.

Regular Updates: Keep updating your journal regularly. This could be weekly or monthly, depending on your preference. Regular entries can help you track your progress and adjust your goals and strategies as needed.

- **Example:** Every Sunday night, review the journal for the week, recording progress on the emotions felt and events that occurred. Evaluate progress towards goals and adjust next week's action plans if necessary.

Seek Feedback: If comfortable, share some of your reflections with a trusted friend or mentor and seek their feedback. They may offer insights that you still need to consider.

- **Example:** Email your monthly reflections to a mentor and consider the next steps based on their feedback. Alternatively, meet with a trusted friend at a café once a month to discuss each other's journals.

Practice Self-Compassion: Remember to be kind to yourself throughout this process. Growth takes time, and it's okay to acknowledge both your successes and areas for improvement.

- **Example:** When you tend to be overly critical of yourself, verbally remind yourself that "you don't need to be perfect." Also, record what you've learned from failures, accepting them as part of growth.

By following these steps, you can use reflective journaling as a tool for self-discovery and personal development.

Mini Actions You Can Take: 6.1

Recognize where you stand on the self-esteem spectrum. Then, using reflective journaling prompts, identify your tendencies in reacting to external matters. Create and implement tools for self-discovery and personal development.

6.2 BREAKING FREE FROM THE NEED FOR EXTERNAL VALIDATION

Relying on external validation can be slippery, leading to instability in your sense of self-worth. When your value hinges on others' approval, you become vulnerable to their opinions, which can change on a whim. This constant need for validation disrupts your personal happiness, making you feel incomplete unless someone else acknowledges your worth. It also impacts your decision-making, as you prioritize pleasing others over what truly makes you happy. This external reliance makes it difficult to trust your judgment, leading to anxiety and self-doubt. Over time, this cycle erodes your self-esteem, making you more susceptible to emotional turmoil.

Transitioning to internal validation requires a conscious shift in mindset. Begin by identifying your personal values and beliefs. Reflect on what truly matters to you, independent of others' opinions. Knowing your values provides a solid foundation for self-worth, allowing you to make decisions that align with your true self. Setting personal goals based on intrinsic motivation is another crucial step. Focus on what you want to achieve for your satisfaction rather than seeking external approval. These internally driven goals give you a sense of purpose and accomplishment, reinforcing your self-worth.

Recognizing and challenging validation-seeking behavior is essential. Start by paying attention to moments when you crave others' approval. Reflective exercises can help you identify these patterns. For instance, keep a journal where you note instances when you seek validation and how it makes you feel. Over time, you'll notice patterns that reveal your triggers. Once you identify these moments, challenge the need for approval with positive self-affirmations. When you catch yourself seeking validation, remind yourself of your worth. Say things like, "I trust my judgment," or "I am enough as I am." These affirmations help shift your focus from external to internal validation, reinforcing your self-worth.

Consider the story of Emily, who constantly sought approval at work. She doubted her abilities and relied on her boss's praise to feel competent. This dependency made her anxious and hesitant to take risks. Emily broke free from this cycle by focusing on her intrinsic motivations. She identified her core values and set personal goals that aligned with them. Emily also sought help from a higher power to remind herself of her capabilities. Over time, she learned to trust her judgment and make decisions confidently. Her anxiety decreased, and she felt more empowered in her career.

Another powerful example is Sarah, who was addicted to social media validation. She checked for likes and comments, tying her self-worth to online approval. Realizing the detrimental impact, Sarah took a social media break. During this time, she practiced being present at the moment and self-validation and focused on activities that brought her joy and fulfillment, independent of others' opinions. Sarah also avoided asking others for validation; instead, she asked the higher power to indicate her inner values and trust her feelings and judgments. This shift allowed her to break free from the cycle of external validation, fostering a stronger sense of self-worth.

Breaking free from the need for external validation is a transformative process. You can cultivate a robust sense of self-worth by identifying your values, setting intrinsic goals, and challenging validation-seeking behaviors. This shift empowers you to trust your judgment, make decisions aligned with your true self, and find happiness from within.

Mini Actions You Can Take: 6.2

Do you find that seeking approval, praise, and admiration from others has become a significant indicator of your happiness? Do you take pleasure in competing to showcase affluence on social media? Envision a scenario where you are required to undergo an extended period of rest, during which you cannot travel, apply makeup, dine out, or dress in high fashion. Where would you seek happiness in such circumstances? If you feel that social media is taking up a considerable amount of your time and energy, you might find it beneficial to reallocate some of that time to personal rejuvenation.

6.3 EMBRACING AUTHENTICITY: BEING TRUE TO YOURSELF

Authenticity is about living in alignment with your actual values and beliefs. It means being genuine in your actions and interactions, allowing your true self to shine through. When you live authentically, you honor your identity and experience deep self-respect. This connection between authenticity and self-respect is vital for building self-worth. Living authentically means acknowledging and embracing yourself rather than trying to fit into someone else's mold. It's about recognizing and valuing your unique qualities, which fosters a strong sense of self-worth and confidence.

However, embracing authenticity is easier said than done. Fear of judgment or rejection often stands in the way. You may worry about what others think or fear that being your authentic self will lead to exclusion or criticism. Societal expectations and pressure add another layer of complexity. Society often dictates specific standards for behavior, appearance, and success. These external pressures can make it challenging to stay true to yourself, as you might feel compelled to conform to avoid standing out or being judged. The need for acceptance can lead you to suppress your true feelings and desires, creating a disconnect between your inner self and outward actions.

To embrace authenticity, start by identifying your core values. Reflect on what truly matters to you and what principles guide your life. These values serve as a compass, helping you navigate decisions and actions in a way that aligns with your true self. Once you clearly understand your values, make a conscious effort to align your actions with them. This alignment ensures that your behavior reflects your true beliefs, fostering a sense of integrity and self-respect. Practicing honesty and transparency in your relationships is another crucial step. Openly expressing your thoughts, feelings, and needs allows you to build genuine connections based on mutual respect and understanding.

Consider the story of Laura, who found her voice in a new career path. For years, Laura worked in a job that didn't fulfill her, feeling pressured to adhere to societal expectations of success. She suppressed her true passion for writing, fearing judgment and financial instability. Eventually, Laura decided to embrace her authenticity. She took a leap of faith and pursued a career in writing. This decision aligned with her core values of creativity and self-expression. Laura felt a profound sense of fulfillment and self-respect as she started writing. Her authenticity boosted her self-worth and led to a successful and satisfying career.

Another inspiring example is Mia, who embraced her individuality through personal style and interests. Mia always felt pressured to conform to fashion trends and societal beauty standards. This pressure made her feel disconnected from her true self. One day, Mia decided to explore her style, regardless of what others thought. She started wearing clothes that made her feel comfortable and confident, embracing her unique taste. Mia also pursued hobbies that genuinely interested her, such as painting and gardening. By living authentically, Mia experienced a newfound sense of self-worth and joy. Her confidence grew, and she felt more connected to her true self and surroundings.

Embracing authenticity requires courage and self-awareness. It means facing judgment and rejection while staying true to your values. To support this journey, surround yourself with supportive and like-minded individuals who appreciate you for who you are. These positive relationships reinforce your self-worth and provide a safe space for authentic expression. Additionally, practice self-compassion. Understand that being true to yourself is a continuous process, and making mistakes along the way is okay. Treat yourself with kindness and patience as you navigate the path to authenticity.

Living authentically transforms your life. It deepens your self-respect, strengthens your self-worth, and fosters genuine connections with others. By identifying your core values, aligning your actions with them, and practicing honesty in your relationships, you can embrace your true self and experience the profound benefits of authenticity. Remember, your uniqueness is your strength, and living authentically allows you to honor and celebrate that uniqueness daily.

Mini Actions You Can Take: 6.3

Understand your priorities. Regularly reaffirm to yourself what's important, such as family, friends, goal-oriented work, and commitments.

Reflect on your core beliefs. Consider values like honesty, not speaking ill of others, avoiding greed, and being mindful of the needs of those around you.

What captivates you? Are there activities that absorb you so profoundly that you lose track of time or find ideas spontaneously arising, even while doing chores or driving? Your life's work can be something other than your full-time job. It could involve volunteering on weekends, writing, or creating videos in your spare time. Remember what you loved doing as a child—there might be clues. Once you have an idea, start taking small steps toward it. Before you know it, you might discover something that captivates and enchants you.

6.4 THE POWER OF POSITIVE AFFIRMATIONS: REWIRING YOUR BRAIN

Positive affirmations have the unique power to rewire your brain and improve self-esteem. The science behind this lies in neuroplasticity, the brain's remarkable ability to change and adapt. Neuroplasticity allows your brain to form new neural connections throughout your life. When you repeat positive affirmations, you train your brain to create and strengthen these new pathways. This process can shift your mindset from one of negativity and self-doubt to one filled with confidence and self-worth.

Positive affirmations work by impacting the neural pathways in your brain. When you consistently repeat positive statements, your brain begins to associate these statements with your core beliefs. Over time, these affirmations become ingrained in your neural circuitry, making them your default mode of thinking. This shift can significantly improve your self-esteem and overall mental health. Studies have shown that positive thinking can lead to increased life span, lower rates of depression, and better psychological well-being. By focusing on positive affirmations, you can harness the power of neuroplasticity to foster a healthier, more optimistic mindset.

Creating effective affirmations is critical to their success. Start by using present tense and positive language. Instead of saying, "I will be confident," say, "I am confident." This phrasing makes the affirmation feel immediate and real, helping your brain to accept it as truth.

Make your affirmations specific and personal. Generic statements like "I am strong." may not resonate as profoundly as "I am capable of handling any challenge that comes my way. I am presented with numerous challenges. However, with each challenge, I am also provided with the ideas, skills, abilities, and help necessary to solve and overcome them. I fear nothing because a great power gives me everything I need."

Tailoring affirmations to your unique experiences and goals gives them more power and relevance.

Incorporating affirmations into your daily routine is important to maximize their impact. Repeating affirmations each morning can set a positive tone for the day. Find a quiet moment to say your affirmations out loud or silently while getting ready to go out or during your morning commute. Consistency is vital; the more you repeat them, the stronger their effect on your brain. Writing affirmations in a journal can also reinforce their power. You engage multiple senses each time you write them down, making the affirmations more tangible and memorable.

Here are some examples of affirmations you can use or adapt to fit your needs:

- "I am worthy of love and respect."
- "I am capable and confident in the abilities given to me."
- "I embrace my unique qualities and strengths."
- "Happiness and success are given to me."
- "I am resilient and can overcome any obstacle."

These affirmations cover various aspects of self-love and self-worth, providing a comprehensive approach to building a positive self-image. Feel free to modify these affirmations to make them more personal and relevant to your experiences and goals.

Positive affirmations can also be a powerful tool during challenging moments. When you face a difficult situation or experience self-doubt, take a moment to repeat your affirmations. This can help ground you and remind you of your worth and capabilities.

For instance, if you're about to start a job interview and feel nervous, repeating the following can boost your confidence and calm your nerves: "The Higher Power resides within me. You have already granted us the utmost power; I will exhibit that supreme power now. I will conclude this interview feeling completely relaxed, ensuring I am clear and persuasive."

Positive affirmations have the power to transform your mindset and improve your self-esteem. Understanding the science behind affirmations and incorporating them into your daily routine can harness the brain's ability to change and create a more positive, empowered self-perception.

Mini Actions You Can Take: 6.4

To make affirmations a part of your daily practice, consider incorporating them into a morning or evening routine.

For example, start your day by standing in front of the mirror and repeating your affirmations with conviction. Visualize yourself embodying these positive statements and notice how they make you feel. Over time, this practice can shift your mindset and help you internalize the affirmations as truth.

Another approach is to write your affirmations on sticky notes and place them where you'll see them frequently, such as on your bathroom mirror, computer screen, or refrigerator. These visual reminders can reinforce the affirmations throughout the day.

CHAPTER 7

BATTLING SOCIAL PRESSURES AND UNREALISTIC EXPECTATIONS

I magine yourself standing in a crowded room, surrounded by people who appear to have everything. Their lives seem perfect, their smiles effortless, and their confidence solid. You look at yourself and wonder why you don't measure up. This pressure to conform to an ideal is a daily reality for many women. Social norms and expectations shape our self-esteem and self-worth, often making us feel inadequate and overwhelmed.

7.1 UNDERSTANDING SOCIETAL PRESSURES: THE IMPACT ON SELF-ESTEEM

Societal pressures are the unwritten rules and expectations that dictate how we should look, behave, and succeed. Cultural standards of beauty, for instance, play a significant role in shaping women's self-esteem. From a young age, we are bombarded with images of what is considered beautiful—flawless skin, a slim figure, and perfect hair. These unrealistic standards create a perpetual cycle of comparison and self-criticism. You might constantly strive to achieve a specific body type, feeling that anything less makes you unworthy. This relentless pursuit of an idealized appearance can lead to negative body image and low self-esteem, as noted in studies on appearance-related social pressure.

Beyond beauty, societal expectations extend to behavior and roles. Women are often pressured to conform to traditional roles, such as nurturing caregivers or efficient homemakers. While there is nothing inherently wrong with these roles, the pressure to fulfill them ideally can be overwhelming. You might feel torn between meeting these expectations and pursuing your dreams and ambitions. The pressure to excel in multiple areas of life—career, family, and social circles—adds another layer of stress. Balancing these demands can leave you feeling stretched thin, constantly questioning your worth and capabilities.

Specific societal pressures further complicate the issue. The pressure to achieve a particular type of body is pervasive and insidious. Whether through media portrayals or societal norms, the message is clear: to be beautiful, you must fit a specific mold. This pressure can lead to unhealthy behaviors, such as extreme dieting or overexercising, in an attempt to conform. The expectation to balance career and family ideally is another standard pressure. You may need to excel at work and be the perfect partner and parent. This unrealistic standard can create feelings of inadequacy and guilt when you inevitably fall short.

Social media adds another layer of complexity. The standards social media influencers and celebrities set can make it seem like everyone else is leading a perfect life. Curated images of success, beauty, and happiness flood your feed, creating a distorted reality. Constantly exposing these idealized portrayals can lead to feelings of inadequacy and self-doubt. You might find yourself comparing your everyday life to the highlight reels of others, wondering why you can't measure up.

The psychological effects of societal pressures are profound. Increased anxiety and stress are common responses to the relentless demands of perfection. You might feel a constant sense of urgency as if you are constantly falling behind. This anxiety can permeate every aspect of your life, affecting your mental and physical health. Feelings of inadequacy and failure often accompany these pressures. When you can't meet the unrealistic standards set by society, it's easy to internalize these failures as personal shortcomings. This can lead to a negative self-image and low self-esteem, making recognizing and appreciating your worth challenging.

Constant comparison and self-criticism are also byproducts of societal pressures. You might find yourself mentally measuring your achievements, appearance, and lifestyle against those of others. This perpetual comparison can erode your self-confidence and reinforce feelings of unworthiness. It's a never-ending cycle where you feel you are never good enough, no matter how much you achieve or how hard you try.

Societal pressures are pervasive and challenging to navigate, but recognizing their impact is the first step towards overcoming them. By understanding how these pressures shape your self-esteem and identifying your specific challenges, you can take proactive steps to protect your mental health and build a more positive self-image.

Mini Actions You Can Take: 7.1

Stop using unreasonable demands at work, enviable beauty, body shapes, or travel stories on social media to measure your worth. Decide for yourself what you want to achieve. Clearly understand where you are now and where you want to be, and do not let others influence this space. Next, decide on the actions you need to take to reach your desired position. The most important thing here is to set small steps to continue to follow.

First, identify the areas you want to improve, such as your physical condition, body shape, eating habits, exercise habits, and sleeping hours. Then, create an action plan to achieve these goals. It's important to start with a manageable plan that can be sustained and gradually progress from there.

- **Example 1:** Stop eating ice cream and snacks after meals. Don't eat anything after 6 PM. If you want to eat, have just one fruit, like an apple, pear, or plum. If you're going to eat ice cream or snacks, allow yourself to do so once a week.
- **Example 2:** Plan to go to the gym three days a week; if you can't make it, do 10 minutes of light exercises like sit-ups, squats, or stretching at home.

Setting a rigorous plan that you can't stick to can undermine your confidence. The key to continual progress is setting and maintaining a more relaxed plan.

7.2 OVERCOMING PERFECTIONISM: EMBRACING GOOD ENOUGH

Perfectionism is the unrealistic pursuit of flawlessness, often driven by a fear of making mistakes or failing. This mindset can be incredibly detrimental to your self-esteem and mental health. When you constantly strive for perfection, you set unattainable standards for yourself. Every minor mistake feels like a significant failure, reinforcing a negative self-image. This relentless pressure can lead to chronic stress, anxiety, and even depression. Perfectionism creates a vicious cycle where the fear of failure paralyzes you, preventing you from taking risks or trying new things.

The roots of perfectionism often trace back to high parental expectations during childhood. If you grew up with parents who demanded excellence in every aspect of your life, you might have internalized the belief that your worth is tied to your achievements. This pressure to excel can follow you into adulthood, making you feel that anything less than perfect is unacceptable.

Societal emphasis on achievement and success further fuels perfectionistic tendencies. We live in a culture that glorifies accomplishments and often equates success with personal value. The constant barrage of success stories and accolades can make you feel that you must continuously prove your worth.

Internalized beliefs about self-worth and performance play a significant role as well. You might believe you are only valuable if you perform flawlessly, leading to a relentless pursuit of perfection.

To overcome perfectionism, it's crucial to set realistic and achievable goals. Start by breaking down your larger goals into smaller, manageable tasks. This approach allows you to celebrate small victories and reduces the pressure to be perfect. For instance, if you're working on a significant project, set daily or weekly milestones you can realistically achieve. This makes the task more manageable and helps build self-trust and confidence.

Another vital strategy is practicing self-compassion when mistakes happen. Understand that everyone makes mistakes, and these errors do not define your worth. Treat yourself with the kindness and understanding you offer a friend when you stumble. Instead of berating yourself for a mistake, acknowledge it, learn from it, and move forward. This shift in mindset can significantly reduce the anxiety and stress associated with perfectionism.

Focusing on progress rather than perfection is also essential. Recognize that growth and improvement are more valuable than achieving an impossible standard. Celebrate the progress you make, no matter how small. For example, if you're learning a new skill, appreciate each step of your journey rather than fixating on becoming an expert overnight. This focus on progress helps you build resilience and encourages a more positive self-view.

Consider the story of Megan, who struggled with perfectionism in her career. She always needed to deliver flawless work, fearing that any mistake would jeopardize her professional reputation. This fear led to long hours, immense stress, and eventual burnout. Megan decided to embrace the concept of "good enough." She began setting realistic goals and allowed herself to make mistakes. Over time, she realized that her worth was not tied to her work's perfection. This acceptance reduced her stress levels and improved her overall well-being, making her more effective and happier in her job.

Another example is Lisa, a mother pressured to be the perfect parent. She believed that any slip-up would harm her children, leading to constant self-criticism and anxiety. Lisa started practicing self-compassion, reminding herself that no parent is perfect and that making mistakes is part of the learning process. She focused on her parenting progress, celebrating small wins like successfully managing a tantrum or creating a fun family activity. This shift in perspective allowed Lisa to embrace her imperfections and thoroughly enjoy her role as a mother.

If you've always believed everything must be perfect or completed 100%, it might be time to reconsider your approach. Remember, Life is full of unexpected challenges, even if you only complete 70% of your tasks on some days or sometimes even less than half. The ability to adapt and persevere is a sign of personal growth. "Today, I'm tired, so I'll rest when I get home" is a perfectly acceptable decision.

Rather than spending excessive time perfecting a single task, prioritizing efficiency can be just as important. An effective strategy is to create an outline and review it after a good night's sleep, which helps you see your tasks more objectively.

Life is akin to mountain climbing. Take the time to enjoy the scenery, rest, breathe in fresh air, and listen to the birds in the greenery. The true goal is to enjoy the journey, not just to reach the summit—if that were the case, taking a helicopter would suffice.

Mini Actions You Can Take: 7.2

Imagine your heart as a heart-shaped cushion. Place it in front of you and give it a gentle massage. As you do, remind yourself, "Let's take it slow. Always chasing perfection can crowd out ease from your heart. Relaxing and smiling make your life more pleasant and enhances the joy of those around you."

7.3 REDEFINING SUCCESS: PERSONAL AND PROFESSIONAL

Success often feels like a predetermined path we must follow, marked by societal measures such as wealth, status, and accolades. However, this traditional definition can leave many feelings fulfilled and constantly chasing an elusive goal. Challenging these conventional definitions and redefining success on your terms is crucial. Success is subjective and deeply personal, varying from one individual to another. Moving away from worldly and societal measures allows you to focus on what truly matters.

Personal success should resonate with your core values and passions. It's about finding fulfillment in achievements that may not necessarily align with society's expectations. For instance, success could mean nurturing meaningful relationships, pursuing a hobby, or dedicating time to personal growth. Aligning success with your values ensures your accomplishments bring genuine happiness and satisfaction. Consider what makes you feel alive and purposeful. Is it creating art, volunteering, or being present for your family? Recognizing and honoring these non-traditional achievements can lead to a more fulfilling life.

In the professional realm, success often hinges on titles and salaries, but this view can be limiting and stressful. Redefining professional success involves looking beyond these external markers. Focus on job satisfaction and work-life balance. A fulfilling career is one where you feel valued, engaged, and excited about your work. It's about making meaningful contributions that align with your values and passions. This approach shifts the emphasis from climbing the corporate ladder to finding a role that resonates with you. Valuing meaningful contributions over accolades allows you to find pride in your impact rather than the recognition you receive.

To help redefine success, try creating a personal success vision board. Gather images, quotes, and symbols representing your unique vision of success. This visual representation will serve as a daily reminder of what you're working towards.

Writing a personal mission statement is another powerful exercise. Outline your core values, passions, and what you want to achieve. This statement can guide your decisions and align you with your true self. Setting values-based career goals is equally important. Identify what you value most in your work and set goals that reflect these priorities. This might mean seeking projects that align with your passions or negotiating a more flexible work schedule.

A personal mission statement reflects an individual's values and goals. Below are four examples of mission statements from different individuals:

- **Health and Happiness Advocate**: "My mission is to enhance lives through health and happiness. I advocate for a balanced diet, regular exercise, and mental health, helping individuals reach their fullest potential."
- **Educational Improvement Teacher**: "My mission is to unlock children's potential through education. I teach passionately and create a supportive environment where learners can confidently expand their knowledge."
- **Environmental Activist**: "My mission is to promote a sustainable Earth. I work with the community to increase environmental protection awareness and implement practical solutions."
- **Artist Inspiring Through Art**: "My mission is to move people emotionally through my art. I capture and express emotions, crafting works that challenge viewers to engage with their feelings and gain new insights and empathy."

These mission statements, rooted in each person's expertise and passion, guide their daily actions and decisions.

Consider the story of Sarah, who left a high-paying corporate job to pursue her passion for writing. She chased promotions and bonuses for years, believing they defined her success. However, the constant stress and lack of fulfillment made her reevaluate her life. Sarah realized that true success for her meant doing what she loved. She transitioned to a career in writing, where she found joy and satisfaction in expressing herself creatively. Though her income was initially lower, the fulfillment she gained was priceless.

Another example is Emma, who found success in achieving work-life balance. Emma had always been ambitious, striving to excel in her career. However, the long hours and constant pressure left her feeling burnt out. She decided to set boundaries and prioritize her well-being. Emma negotiated a flexible work schedule, allowing her to spend more time with her family and engage in activities she loved. This shift improved her mental health and made her more productive and engaged. Emma discovered that success wasn't about working the most extended hours but finding a balance that allowed her to thrive in all aspects of her life.

Redefining success is recognizing that your worth is not tied to external measures. It's about aligning your achievements with your values and passions, finding fulfillment in non-traditional accomplishments, and seeking a balance that allows you to thrive personally and professionally. You can create a truly fulfilling and meaningful life by challenging conventional definitions and embracing your unique vision of success.

Mini Actions You Can Take: 7.3

Create your mission statement. It doesn't need to be tied to your job. Consider what you're passionate about and how continuing to pursue this interest could positively impact those around you.

7.4 EMPOWERMENT THROUGH SELF-WORTH: TOOLS FOR RESILIENCE

Self-worth is the bedrock of resilience. When you value yourself, you build a foundation of mental and emotional strength that helps you withstand societal pressures. Knowing your worth

isn't about arrogance or self-importance; it's about recognizing your inherent value and treating yourself with the respect you deserve. This self-awareness empowers you to bounce back from setbacks more effectively. When faced with challenges, your self-worth stabilizes, reminding you that you can overcome difficulties.

Before learning how to boost resilience and adaptability in adversity, it's essential to understand a key concept. When faced with difficulties, adversities, challenges, or hardships, it is crucial not to avoid them but to confront them directly. In other words, always remember to face challenges head-on, calmly work your way through them, and systematically overcome each obstacle one at a time.

To enhance self-worth, practicing self-affirmations and positive self-talk is crucial. These tools help rewire your brain to focus on your strengths and positive qualities. Start each day with affirmations like, "I'm given the ability, physical strength, skills, and solutions to handle all my daily tasks and problems because a greater power has promised me so. I will not encounter any difficulties. The next step I must take is always revealed to me." Repeating these statements reinforces a positive self-image and helps counteract negative thoughts. When facing setbacks, remind yourself of your successes and the strengths that helped you get through them.

Setting personal goals and achieving them is a powerful way to build self-worth. Goals provide direction and a sense of purpose and achieving them brings a feeling of accomplishment. Start with small, manageable goals that align with your passions and values. Each goal you achieve, no matter how small, will boost your confidence and strengthen your self-worth. These successes accumulate, creating a positive cycle of achievement and self-belief. Whether learning new skills, completing projects, or improving personal habits, each achieved goal is proof of your capabilities.

Engaging in activities that build confidence also enhances self-worth. Participating in hobbies and activities that bring joy, and fulfillment can significantly impact self-esteem. Activities like painting, dancing, gardening, or playing sports allow for self-expression and provide opportunities to experience success in different areas of life. They also offer chances to connect with others with similar interests, further boosting your sense of belonging and self-worth. These positive experiences build up, forming a reserve of confidence that you can draw on in difficult times.

Having a solid support system is crucial for developing resilience and self-worth. Being surrounded by positive influences provides emotional support and encouragement. Seek out friends, family, or mentors who uplift and inspire you. Their faith in your abilities can reinforce your self-belief. Mentorship is incredibly impactful, providing guidance and perspectives that help you navigate life's challenges. The support from a mentor is an invaluable resource that offers insights for personal and professional growth.

Consider the story of Anna. She faced a significant personal setback when her long-term relationship ended. Initially, she felt lost and believed she had no value. However, Anna decided to focus on rebuilding her self-worth. She began practicing daily affirmations, reminding herself of her strengths and positive qualities. She set small, achievable goals like a new hobby or volunteering at a local charity. These activities gave her a sense of purpose and fulfillment. Additionally, she leaned on her support network and sought advice from a trusted mentor. Over time, Anna's self-worth grew, and she found resilience in facing her challenges.

Another example is Maria, who struggled with self-doubt after a career setback. She felt overwhelmed and questioned her abilities. Maria decided to focus on activities that brought her joy and confidence. She joined a community theater group, where she discovered a passion for acting. The positive feedback from her peers boosted her confidence. Maria also set and achieved personal goals, such as completing a professional certification. Her support network, including friends and mentors, provided encouragement and guidance. Through these efforts, Maria rebuilt her self-worth and resilience, eventually finding success and satisfaction in her career.

Building self-worth and resilience is a dynamic process that involves self-affirmation, goal-setting, engaging in confidence-building activities, and leveraging support systems. By cultivating these practices, you empower yourself to face societal pressures with strength and confidence, knowing that you are worthy and capable of overcoming any challenge.

Mini Actions You Can Take: 7.4

In the morning, stand in front of the mirror and say, "I have nothing to fear. I have already been given the solutions to today's tasks and problems. With confidence and composure, I will navigate through the day."

In the next chapter, we'll explore how to cultivate a holistic approach to well-being, integrating emotional, mental, and physical practices to foster self-love and resilience. This comprehensive approach will give you the tools to maintain balance and harmony in all aspects of your life.

CHAPTER 8

CULTIVATING A HOLISTIC APPROACH TO HAPPINESS

I magine starting each day feeling balanced and complete, regardless of the challenges life presents. Picture yourself handling daily tasks with calmness and clarity. Knowing you have the means to manage whatever happens is the essence of a holistic approach to happiness. It's about integrating emotional, mental, and physical health into daily practices to achieve a harmonious balance. This chapter begins with the foundations of emotional well-being and offers strategies to develop this comprehensive approach.

8.1 EMOTIONAL WELL-BEING: PRACTICES FOR EMOTIONAL HEALTH

Emotional well-being is a crucial component of overall well-being. Think of your emotions as signals—like a traffic light system—guiding you through your day. When you feel joy, it's a green light, encouraging you to move forward. When you feel anger, it's a red light urging you to pause and assess the situation. Emotional health impacts every aspect of your daily life and relationships. It influences how you interact with others, how you handle stress, and how you perceive yourself. Understanding and managing your emotions allows you to navigate life with greater ease and resilience.

One effective way to enhance emotional well-being is through journaling. This practice allows you to process your thoughts and feelings, providing clarity and insight into your emotional state. Start by setting aside a few minutes daily to write about your experiences, emotions, and reflections. You don't need to worry about grammar or structure—just let your thoughts flow freely. Journaling helps you become more aware of your emotions and can reduce anxiety by breaking the cycle of obsessive thinking. It also encourages openness and can promote reaching out for social support when needed.

Engaging in regular emotional check-ins is another powerful practice. Take a moment each day to ask yourself how you are feeling. Are you stressed, happy, anxious, or content? By regularly checking in with your emotions, you can better understand your needs and take appropriate actions to address them. This practice helps you stay connected to your emotional state and prevents feelings from building up and becoming overwhelming. Emotional check-ins can be as simple as pausing for a few minutes in the morning or evening to reflect on your day and how you felt during different moments.

Expressing your emotions in healthy ways is vital for emotional well-being. Bottling up feelings can lead to increased stress and emotional turmoil. Find outlets that allow you to express what you're feeling. Talking to a trusted friend or therapist can provide a safe space to share your thoughts and gain perspective. Sometimes, verbalizing your emotions can offer relief and clarity.

Creative outlets like art or music are also excellent ways to express emotions. Painting, drawing, or playing an instrument allows you to channel your feelings into a tangible form, providing a sense of release and understanding.

Spend time with friends who allow you to express your emotions freely and share your thoughts without reservation. Talking loudly, having long conversations, and laughing can significantly relieve stress. If you find yourself alone every day, not talking or laughing with anyone or expressing your thoughts, gradually try to start meeting with friends. If you have much time alone, watch comedies and laugh, or call your friend and try to talk and laugh as much as possible. Crying can also relieve stress. If you have been suppressing your emotions, keeping them locked in a box for a long time, finding the courage to open it, confront your feelings, and cry your heart out. After a good cry, you'll notice how much clearer your feelings become. Not just about your own experiences, watching a moving film and letting yourself cry freely can also help alleviate stress.

Consider the story of Jane, who used art therapy to process her grief after losing a loved one. She found it difficult to articulate her emotions through words, but she could express her sadness and pain through painting. Each brushstroke helped her release some of her weight, and she began feeling lighter and more hopeful. Art therapy combines the creative process with psychotherapy, facilitating self-exploration and understanding. It provides a unique way to cope with grief and other intense emotions, offering a relaxing and healing experience.

Art therapy is psychotherapy that enhances emotional health through creative expressions like painting, sculpture, music, and dance. This form of therapy aims to deepen participants' self-expression, help them visualize their internal thoughts and feelings, and aid in the release of mental stress and trauma. Professional therapists typically conduct art therapy and include various art activities customized to meet individual needs.

Benefits of Art Therapy:

- **Emotional Expression:** Art can be a tool for expressing difficult-to-verbal emotions and experiences. This facilitates the surfacing and processing of suppressed feelings and trauma.
- **Stress Reduction:** Participating in creative activities has a calming effect, which can significantly reduce stress.
- **Improved Self-Awareness:** By creating art, individuals can explore their inner selves and enhance their self-awareness.

Practical Examples of Art Therapy:

- **Painting:**
  - **Materials:** Canvas, acrylic paints, brushes.
  - **Method:** Choose colors freely and use them to express your current emotions on the canvas. Concentrate on the color flow and brush movements without focusing on forming specific shapes.
- **Clay Sculpting:**
  - **Materials:** Clay.
  - **Method:** Shape clay into an object that symbolizes your current emotions. This activity transforms feelings into a tangible form, helping you understand them more clearly.

- **Collage:**
  - **Materials:** Magazines, scissors, glue, paper.
  - **Method:** Cut out images and words from magazines that resonate with your emotions and arrange them on paper to form a cohesive artwork. This process helps visualize and organize your internal feelings and thoughts.
- **Music Therapy:**
  - **Method:** Listen to your favorite music in a relaxed state or play an instrument. Choose soothing music and let yourself be carried away by the emotional flow of the tunes.

These activities allow participants to find new ways of expressing themselves and learn techniques to support their emotional health. While art therapy is commonly facilitated by a professional, individuals can also begin with simple activities independently.

Another example is Emily, who managed her daily stress through regular emotional check-ins. She started each morning by taking a few minutes to assess her emotional state. If she felt anxious, she practiced deep breathing exercises or took a short walk to clear her mind. These check-ins helped her stay attuned to her needs and prevented stress from accumulating. By addressing her emotions early, Emily found she could easily navigate her day and maintain balance.

Incorporating these practices into your daily routine can enhance your emotional well-being and create a solid foundation for overall health. Emotional awareness through journaling, regular check-ins, and healthy emotional expression are critical components of a holistic approach to well-being. They help you understand and manage your emotions, leading to improved mental health and more fulfilling relationships.

Mini Actions You Can Take: 8.1

Stop holding back your emotions. Let them out. Express yourself through talking, writing, laughing, crying, or art. You'll feel lighter and more refreshed.

8.2 MENTAL CLARITY: TECHNIQUES FOR MENTAL WELL-BEING

Mental clarity is like a clear blue sky after a storm. It brings calm and direction, allowing you to navigate your day with confidence and focus. A clear and focused mind is essential for well-being because it enhances decision-making and boosts productivity. When your mind is cluttered, it's like trying to find your way through a dense fog. Everything feels overwhelming, and even the most straightforward decisions can become daunting.

One effective way to achieve mental clarity is through mindfulness. Mindfulness involves paying attention to the present moment without judgment. It's about being fully engaged in whatever you are doing. Over time, this practice can help reduce mental clutter and increase your ability to concentrate.

Another technique to clear your mind is engaging in mental decluttering exercises. Just as you would declutter your physical space, you can declutter your mind. Start by identifying the thoughts that are taking up unnecessary space. Are you worried about things beyond your control? Are you holding onto past regrets? Write these thoughts down to externalize them, making it easier to let go. Once you've identified the sources of mental clutter, implement strategies to reduce them. This could involve setting boundaries, prioritizing tasks, or practicing mindfulness to stay present.

Mental clutter can significantly impact your well-being. It can lead to stress and overwhelm, making it difficult to focus on what truly matters. By recognizing the sources of mental clutter, you can take steps to address them. For instance, if you find that social media is a significant source of distraction, consider a digital detox. Limit your screen time and allocate specific periods during the day for checking messages and browsing. This simple change can free up mental space, allowing you to focus on more meaningful activities.

For many years, Sarah felt overwhelmed by regrets about the past, distracted by the actions and words of those around her, and burdened by intrusive thoughts. These distractions filled her mind like clutter, preventing her from focusing on her work and enjoying her private time. However, Sarah decided to try mindfulness, focusing intently on her current tasks and clearing the mental clutter.

As a result of her mindfulness practice, Sarah's mind became like a minimalist room, free of unnecessary items and organized with only what was needed. This newfound clarity dramatically improved her work productivity and created ample time for her to think about and enjoy her activities. In her mind, visualized as a minimalist space, there were only essential items like a table, chair, bed, and refrigerator, each clearly defined and appreciated.

Another example is Emma, who is overwhelmed by the constant influx of information from her phone and computer. She decided to try a digital detox by setting specific times to check her devices. Emma turned off notifications and dedicated certain hours as screen-free periods. This change allowed her to declutter her mind and be more present in her daily activities. She noticed a significant improvement in her mental well-being and found it easier to concentrate on tasks without the constant distraction of digital noise.

These stories illustrate that achieving mental clarity is possible with practical techniques and consistent effort. By practicing mindfulness, engaging in mental decluttering exercises, and recognizing sources of mental clutter, you can create a more transparent, focused mind. This clarity enhances decision-making, boosts productivity, and improves overall well-being.

Mini Actions You Can Take: 8.2

In a typical 24-hour day, assume you spend eight hours sleeping and working and four hours on necessary daily activities such as eating, household chores, commuting, and getting ready. This leaves four hours for you. During this time, clear your mind of unnecessary information and worries and define what you would like to achieve in these four hours.

8.3 PHYSICAL SELF-CARE: HOW TO KEEP YOUR BODY IN THE BEST CONDITION

Today's prevalent health issues, such as obesity, insomnia, lethargy, distractibility, and depression, are primarily caused by chronic inflammation—a process of prolonged damage repair that often remains undetected.

Obesity, for instance, is essentially a constant battle against visceral fat. Effectively managing inflammation is vital because it strengthens the immune system, our primary defense against illness.

Factors like excessive caloric intake, lack of sleep, inadequate exercise, and insufficient mental and emotional rest contribute to weakened immunity and the rise of modern diseases.

Regulate Your Gut:

The gut plays a vital role in the immune system. Antibiotics can destroy a third of the beneficial bacteria in the gut, and it takes about six months to recover, so it's best to use them sparingly. Probiotics are beneficial for increasing good bacteria, and it's also recommended to regularly consume fermented foods and dietary fibers to nourish these bacteria.

Fermented Foods

- Yogurt - A dairy product made by fermenting milk with a yogurt culture.
- Sauerkraut - Fermented cabbage, common in German cuisine.
- Kimchi - A Korean dish made from fermented vegetables, primarily napa cabbage and Korean radishes, mixed with various seasonings.
- Kombucha - A fermented, lightly effervescent, sweetened black or green tea drink.
- Miso - A Japanese seasoning produced by fermenting soybeans with salt and koji mold, often used in soups.
- Tempeh - Made from fermented soybeans, it's a popular protein source, particularly in Indonesian cuisine.
- Kefir - Fermented milk drink similar to yogurt but with a thinner consistency. It originates from the North Caucasus.
- Pickles - Cucumbers or other vegetables fermented in brine or vinegar, prevalent in many cultures worldwide.
- Sourdough Bread - Bread made from the naturally occurring yeast and bacteria in flour.
- Natto - A traditional Japanese food made from soybeans fermented with Bacillus subtilis var. natto.

Dietary fiber is an essential part of a healthy diet, contributing to digestion, weight management, and lowering the risk of various diseases. Here are some excellent sources of dietary fiber:

1. **Whole Grains**:
   - Oats
   - Barley
   - Quinoa
   - Brown rice
   - Whole wheat products (bread, pasta)
2. **Legumes**:
   - Lentils

- Black beans
- Chickpeas
- Kidney beans
- Peas

3. **Nuts and Seeds**:
   - Almonds
   - Chia seeds
   - Flaxseeds
   - Walnuts
   - Sunflower seeds

4. **Vegetables**:
   - Broccoli
   - Carrots
   - Brussels sprouts
   - Sweet potatoes
   - Artichokes

5. **Fruits**:
   - Apples (with skin)
   - Pears (with skin)
   - Bananas
   - Oranges

6. **Berries**:
   - Blueberries
   - Strawberries
   - Blackberries
   - Raspberries

Including a variety of these foods in your diet can help ensure you're getting a good mix of soluble and insoluble fiber, both of which play important roles in health.

Avoid fast food, snacks, and sugary drinks as they are high in fats and carbohydrates, including trans fats—hydrogenated vegetable oils that are cheap and stable but can exacerbate poor gut health and contribute to various health issues.

Environmental design determines behavior:

Google conducted an internal study on environmental design. They found that when a salad bar was placed near the entrance of the company cafeteria, more employees chose salads than when it was placed further away.

Similarly, when snacks like nuts and chips were placed next to the drink bar, more people picked up snacks than when these were placed farther away.

This example shows that we can effectively transform bad habits into good ones by organizing our environment. For instance, if there's a fast food place you often stop by on your way home from work, changing your route to avoid it can help prevent this habit.

Also, not keeping items like juice, chips, alcohol, chocolate, and ice cream at home can prevent overeating and excessive drinking. A good rule to follow is only to go out and buy these items when you want them. This reduces the stress of resisting temptation, and often, the inconvenience of going out just for these items leads to healthier choices like opting for unsweetened soda water instead of cola, crispy dried apples instead of chips, yogurt instead of ice cream, and non-alcoholic beer instead of alcohol. This can then become a habit.

Connecting with Nature:

Modern individuals spend too little time in contact with nature.

Spending time in nature can activate the parasympathetic nervous system (the nerve dominant during relaxation) and reduce inflammation. Therefore, understanding the hormonal balance in your body is crucial.

Key Hormones:

- Dopamine: The excitement and pleasure hormone
- Adrenaline: The alert and threat response hormone
- Oxytocin: The satisfaction and safety hormone

Modern life often involves alternating between excitement and alertness. For example, getting upset while reading social media after a party can trigger these responses.

Oxytocin is often lacking in modern life. Simple actions like changing your PC's wallpaper to a natural scene, hanging photos of nature on your walls, or placing houseplants can help. Walking in the park or spending weekends in areas rich in nature, like forests, beaches, or riversides, provides the necessary rest for the mind and heart.

Talk and Laugh with Friends:

Conversations with trusted friends can stimulate the release of oxytocin, reducing stress and promoting feelings of well-being.

Good Posture:

Posture and confidence are closely related. Research has shown that maintaining an upright posture, with your back straight and chest out, reduces the stress hormone cortisol and increases testosterone, which is responsible for motivation and drive. Start cultivating the habit of consistently being mindful of your posture from today.

Sleep Well:

Criteria for Quality Sleep:

- Fall asleep within 30 minutes of going to bed.
- Wake up no more than once during the night.
- If you do wake up, fall back asleep within 20 minutes.

Improving Sleep Quality

Avoid using your phone and keep your room dark to help you fall asleep. Consider the following tips if you can't sleep after an hour in bed. During sleep, your body alternates between non-REM (deep sleep) and REM (light sleep) about three to four times. The first cycle of non-REM sleep is vital, helping detoxify the brain, rejuvenate the skin, and solidify memories.

Pre-sleep Routine

Taking a bath 90 minutes before bed can be beneficial. Soaking in hot water for at least 15 minutes raises your body's core temperature. As your body cools down, it triggers sleepiness because the drop in core temperature signals to the brain that it's time to sleep. This is supported by research from The Stanford University Sleep Medicine Center. Relaxing your brain before bed is crucial for deep, quality sleep. Balancing your sympathetic (active during the day) and parasympathetic (active during rest) nervous systems by avoiding bright lights, work, and stimulating activities before bed is essential. Ensure your environment supports good sleep by maintaining consistent sleep and wake times and reducing exposure to bright screens at night.

Relaxing your brain before bed is crucial for achieving deep, high-quality sleep.

The human body operates best when there's a balance between the sympathetic nervous system, which is active during the day, and the parasympathetic nervous system, which kicks in during rest. Before bed, promoting activity in the parasympathetic nervous system is important.

To achieve this, you should establish key habits: set consistent sleep and wake times, avoid work, think about stressful topics, and exposure to bright lights before bed.

Using your phone before sleep is a typical modern habit that disrupts sleep.

Eating less and refraining from alcohol before bed are crucial for quality sleep. Both overeating and drinking alcohol can detract from the quality of your sleep.

Regulating Melatonin:

Melatonin, a hormone that promotes sleep, is typically secreted at night but its release is influenced by sunlight exposure during the day.

Adequate daylight exposure ensures that melatonin is released at the right time at night, which enhances sleep quality. At night, avoid bright lights from lamps, computers, and smartphones.

Studies have shown that daylight exposure during the day leads to deeper and more continuous sleep at night. This is because daytime light exposure helps normalize your nighttime sleep cycle. Sunlight not only aids in vitamin D synthesis but also improves overall mood and reduces stress. These benefits can further enhance nighttime sleep quality.

Getting sufficient sunlight can be easily incorporated into your daily routine by spending time outdoors on sunny days, working near a window, or engaging in outdoor activities like walking or light exercise. While morning light is especially beneficial, getting sunlight in the afternoon is also advantageous. In this way, sunlight exposure during the day is vital for promoting and maintaining healthy sleep patterns.

Remember the importance of sleep and commit to getting enough quality rest. Doing so will likely enhance your focus, endurance, decision-making, vitality, and physical strength during the day.

Diet and Exercise:

Eating lightly and avoiding alcohol before bed can improve sleep quality. Daytime exposure to sunlight helps regulate the production of melatonin, the hormone that promotes sleep and enhances nighttime sleep quality. These strategies are all light exercises like walking or stretching that can also improve sleep by promoting physical fatigue and reducing stress. vital to ensuring restorative sleep, which can significantly improve daytime alertness, endurance, decision-making capabilities, vitality, and overall physical strength.

These activities can boost metabolism, relieve stress, and stimulate the brain. Intense workouts aren't necessary; moderate exercise twice a week until you sweat lightly can make a noticeable difference.

Mini Actions You Can Take: 8.3

- Maintain good posture.
- Eat less and regularly consume dietary fiber and fermented foods.
- Walk in natural light.
- Do light strength exercises.
- If you take longer than 20 minutes to fall asleep each night, try taking a 15-minute warm bath 90 minutes before bedtime.

These small daily actions can help maintain optimal health by harnessing natural processes and contemporary health insights.

8.4 CREATING A SUPPORTIVE ENVIRONMENT: SURROUNDING YOURSELF WITH POSITIVITY

The environment you live in plays a significant role in your overall well-being. Think of it as the backdrop to your daily life; it can either uplift or drag you down. A positive environment contributes to emotional and mental health by creating a space where you feel safe, supported, and inspired. When your surroundings are filled with positive influences and support systems, practicing self-love and maintaining a healthy mindset becomes easier. Your environment can act like a cushion, softening the blows of life's challenges and providing a sanctuary where you can recharge.

One of the first steps in creating a supportive environment is decluttering and organizing your physical spaces. Clutter can create a sense of chaos and overwhelm, making it difficult to relax and focus. Start by going through your belongings and removing items that no longer serve you. Organize your space in a functional and calming way. This doesn't mean you need a perfectly tidy home but a space that brings you peace. A clean, organized environment can clear your mind and make room for positivity.

Surrounding yourself with positive and supportive people is equally important. Relationships have a profound impact on your self-esteem and overall well-being. Spend time with individuals who uplift and encourage you rather than those who drain your energy. This might mean reevaluating some of your relationships and setting boundaries where necessary. Seek out friendships and connections based on mutual respect and positivity. Engaging with supportive people creates a network of encouragement and strength, helping you navigate life's ups and downs with greater resilience.

Creating a personal sanctuary within your home can also enhance your well-being. This is a space where you can retreat to relax, reflect, and recharge. It could be a cozy corner with a comfortable chair, soft lighting, and your favorite books. Or it's a spot in your garden where you can connect with nature. The key is to make this space your own —a place where you feel completely at ease. Having a sanctuary provides a physical reminder to take time for yourself, promoting self-love and relaxation.

Community and support networks play a crucial role in maintaining well-being. Building and nurturing positive relationships within your community can provide a sense of belonging and support. Join groups or clubs that align with your interests and values. Participate in community events and activities where you can meet like-minded individuals. Online forums and social media groups can also offer support, especially if you want a specific type of connection. These networks provide:

- A platform for sharing experiences.
- Gaining advice.
- Offering encouragement to one another.

Consider the story of Rachel, who transformed her home into a peaceful retreat. After years of feeling overwhelmed by her cluttered living space, she decided to make a change. Rachel started by decluttering each room, donating items she no longer needed, and organizing her belongings. She created a cozy reading nook with soft pillows and warm lighting. This space became her sanctuary, where she could unwind after a long day. The transformation not only improved the aesthetics of her home but also significantly enhanced her mental and emotional well-being.

Another example is Emily, who built a supportive social circle for encouragement and growth. Emily had always struggled with feelings of isolation and low self-esteem. She joined a local book club and a chair exercise class, where she met people who shared her interests. These connections blossomed into meaningful friendships. Emily found herself surrounded by positive influences who encouraged her personal growth. The support from her new friends helped her build confidence and self-love, making a profound difference in her life.

Mini Actions You Can Take: 8.4

Creating a supportive environment is about positively surrounding yourself in every aspect of your life. Declutter your physical spaces, surround yourself with supportive people, and create a personal sanctuary. Engage with your community and build networks that uplift and encourage you. These steps contribute to a nurturing environment that fosters self-love and well-being. These actions create a strong foundation for a balanced and fulfilling life where you can thrive and grow.

WITH GRATITUDE, I INVITE YOU TO HELP OTHERS THROUGH YOUR WORDS!

"The purpose of human life is to serve, and to show compassion and the will to help others."

— ALBERT SCHWEITZER

Imagine a world that is a touch more understanding and compassionate. What if a simple act of yours could contribute to that vision? Today, I invite you to be part of such a change.

Can you support a fellow woman who is perhaps facing challenges similar to the ones you've encountered? She may be overcoming doubts, rebuilding self-esteem, or healing from past hurts—challenges you might recognize. She stands to gain immensely from the empowering insights in "The Power of Self-Love for Women."

Our aim is to illuminate the path to inner peace and happiness for as many as possible, and your review could significantly broaden our reach. Here is my humble request for your support:

Please share your thoughts on this book by leaving a review. This small gesture could have a profound impact on another woman's journey towards:

- Embracing self-love,
- Healing emotional wounds,
- Building confidence,
- Achieving enduring happiness.

To leave your review, simply scan the QR code below:

Thank you for considering this request. I am eager to continue sharing valuable strategies and insights with you to help others discover the courage to embrace self-love.

With heartfelt appreciation and respect,

- Miyuki Sugiura

AFTERWORD

If you chose this book, it's likely because past hurts—perhaps inflicted by family, friends, organizations, or even through interactions on social media—still affect you. You may be grappling with unresolved issues, feeling guilty about past errors, or habitually placing the needs of others before your own. You might struggle to articulate your desires or feel confident in your appearance, personality, or abilities. It's common for those needing self-love to be sensitive and prioritize others over themselves.

I wrote this book to help you prioritize what you want, regain your sense of self, and approach each day with renewed confidence and happiness. At the end of each subchapter, you'll find the suggested "Mini Actions You Can Take". You don't need to try all of them; choose the ones that resonate with you and start there. I would be thrilled if these actions became part of your new routine.

Make a promise to yourself: commit to treating yourself with the same care and love that you show your cherished family and friends. This commitment will guide you to make clear choices and fulfill your needs.

And finally, remember this: You are a unique masterpiece, one of a kind in this world. You are precious. You have the strength, skills, guidance, wisdom, and support needed to overcome any challenges life brings your way. When you seek it, the higher power will provide everything you need. You are never alone on your journey.

Stand tall, keep smiling, and let your days overflow with joy and happiness!

I am deeply grateful to have been a part of your journey toward self-love.

So do not fear, for I am with you; do not be dismayed, for I am your God. I will strengthen you and help you; I will uphold you with my righteous right hand.

— ‹ISAIAH 41:10›

REFERENCES

BetterHelp. (2024 July 22). The importance of setting boundaries for your mental health. Retrieved from https://www.betterhelp.com/advice/general/the-importance-of-setting-boundaries-10-benefits-for-you-and-your-relationships/

BetterUp. (2024 May 23). 60 positive affirmation examples to use daily. Retrieved from https://www.betterup.com/blog/positive-affirmations

Bishop, G. J. (2017, August 1). *Unfuk Yourself: Get Out of Your Head and Into Your Life**. HarperOne.

Brach, T. (2013, January 22). *True Refuge: Finding Peace and Freedom in Your Own Awakened Heart*. Bantam.

Brown, B. (2010, August 27). *The Gifts of Imperfection: Let Go of Who You Think You're Supposed to Be and Embrace Who You Are*. Hazelden.

Carnegie, D. (1936, October 1). *How to Win Friends and Influence People*. Simon & Schuster.

Cascio, C. N., O'Donnell, M. B., Tinney, F. J., Lieberman, M. D., Taylor, S. E., Strecher, V. J., & Falk, E. B. (2016, April). Self-affirmation activates brain systems associated with self-related processing and reward and is reinforced by future orientation. Retrieved from https://www.ncbi.nlm.nih.gov/pmc/articles/PMC4814782/

Church, D., & Brooks, A. J. (2019, February 19). Clinical EFT (Emotional Freedom Techniques) improves multiple physiological markers of health. Retrieved from https://www.ncbi.nlm.nih.gov/pmc/articles/PMC6381429/

Covey, S. R. (1989, August 15). *The 7 Habits of Highly Effective People: Powerful Lessons in Personal Change*. Simon & Schuster.

Doyle, G. (2020, March 10). *Untamed*. The Dial Press.

Frankl, V. E. (1946, September 29). *Man's Search for Meaning*. Beacon Press.

Hamilton, D. R. (2017, February 7). *I Heart Me: The Science of Self-Love*. Hay House.

Healthline. (2020, June 27). Positive self-talk: Benefits and techniques. Retrieved from https://www.healthline.com/health/positive-self-talk

Holliday, R., Diedrichs, P. C., & Gillen, K. (2013, May 17). The face of appearance-related social pressure: Gender, age, body mass index, race, and media consumption patterns. Retrieved from https://www.ncbi.nlm.nih.gov/pmc/articles/PMC3662600/

Kahneman, D. (2011, October 25). *Thinking, Fast and Slow*. Farrar, Straus and Giroux.

Lowe, L. (2023, October 30). 75 Brene Brown quotes on self-love, courage. *Parade*. Retrieved from https://parade.com/1018534/lindsaylowe/brene-brown-quotes/

Medium. (2023, May 11). How to use visualization for increased confidence. Retrieved from https://medium.com/lampshade-of-illumination/how-to-use-visualization-for-increased-confidence-techniques-for-creating-mental-images-that-a92a24f507f0

Molinary, R. (2010, September 7). *Beautiful You: A Daily Guide to Radical Self-Acceptance.* Seal Press.

Neff, K. D. (n.d.). Self-compassion research. Retrieved from https://self-compassion.org/the-research/

Neff, K., & Germer, C. K. (2018, August 14). *The Mindful Self-Compassion Workbook: A Proven Way to Accept Yourself, Build Inner Strength, and Thrive.* Guilford Press.

PositivePsychology.com. (2019, June 18). 14 benefits of practicing gratitude (Incl. Journaling). Retrieved from https://positivepsychology.com/benefits-of-gratitude/

Psychology Today. (2024, March 19). 7 key strategies to overcome perfectionism. Retrieved from https://www.psychologytoday.com/us/blog/mindful-dating/202403/7-key-strategies-to-overcome-perfectionism

Rising Phoenix Wellness Services. (2023, October 18). Childhood trauma: 10 great treatments to help heal. Retrieved from https://www.risingphoenixaz.com/blog/healing-childhood-trauma-recovery/

Robbins, T. (1991, November 1). *Awaken the Giant Within: How to Take Immediate Control of Your Mental, Emotional, Physical and Financial Destiny!.* Free Press.

Rinzler, L., & Watterson, M. (2015, September 15). *How to Love Yourself (and Sometimes Other People).* Hay House.

Seeking Integrity. (2023, July 4). Have you crossed the line? A list of common boundary violations. Retrieved from https://seekingintegrity.com/blog/have-you-crossed-the-line-a-list-of-common-boundary-violations/

Sincero, J. (2013, April 23). *You Are a Badass: How to Stop Doubting Your Greatness and Start Living an Awesome Life.* Running Press Adult.

Tolle, E. (1999, September 27). *The Power of Now: A Guide to Spiritual Enlightenment.* New World Library.

Verywell Mind. (2023, March 23). How does your environment affect your mental health? Retrieved from https://www.verywellmind.com/how-your-environment-affects-your-mental-health-5093687

Made in the USA
Las Vegas, NV
01 February 2025

17363269R00085